Maurice Hageman

What became of Parker

A Farce-comedy in four Acts

Maurice Hageman

What became of Parker
A Farce-comedy in four Acts

ISBN/EAN: 9783337054946

Printed in Europe, USA, Canada, Australia, Japan

Cover: Foto ©ninafisch / pixelio.de

More available books at **www.hansebooks.com**

What Became of Parker

.

A FARCE-COMEDY IN FOUR ACTS

BY

MAURICE HAGEMAN.

Author of Hector—A Crazy Idea—First Kiss—By Telephone—
Mrs. Mulcahy—To Rent—Prof. Robinson
Hageman's Make-up Book—Etc.

CHICAGO
THE DRAMATIC PUBLISHING COMPANY.

Cast of Characters.

Fred Parker, a wholesale dry goods merchant.
William Torrence, his partner.
Jeremiah Growler, a retired business man
James Jones.
Mr. Harrison, a capitalist from Chicago.
Dr. Rogers.
Police-Sergeant Ripley.
Otto, a waiter.

Vivian, Parker's wife.
Mildred Green, her maiden aunt.
Hebe Worthy, Growler's niece.
Cora, maid at Parkers.

The action of the first act takes place in Parker's apartments, Chicago. The following acts are laid at the Park Hotel in Waukesha.

PLAYS TWO AND ONE-HALF HOURS.

Copyright 1898 by the Dramatic Publishing Company, Chicago.

Notice.

What Became of Parker

ACT I.

SCENE: *Room in Parker's flat, furnished to denote comfortable circumstances.* Fred *and* Vivian *discovered.*

Vivian. [*Occupied with some embroidery, seated L.*] Fred, Fred, dear!

Fred. [*Seated R. absorbed in the reading of a newspaper, without looking up.*] Eh?

Vivian. [*Aside.*] He won't pay any attention to me! [*Aloud.*] Fred, it's after ten.

Fred. [*Aside.*] This is getting tiresome! [*Aloud.*] Can't you see that I am busy?

Vivian. [*Smiling.*] Why, you are only reading the newspaper!

Fred. "Only reading the newspaper!" It's of the greatest importance to me; a merchant, above all others, must know what is going on in the world.

Vivian. [*Rising and approaching him.*] Thanks for the information, dear! [*Looks at the paper over Fred's shoulder.*] Only, I was not aware that the reading of the serial story was necessary for your mercantile information. [*Laughs.*] Ha-ha-ha.

Fred. It seems to me you are getting slightly sarcastic of late, Vivian! I suppose that's the result of being so much in the company of your venerable aunt!

Vivian. Oh, poor, innocent aunt Mildred!

Fred. She's a confounded nuisance around here, and I wish she'd leave us alone.

Vivian. I am glad to have her company. What would I do all alone the live long day, while you are at the office?

Fred. I don't know! It seems to me that a woman who is keeping house can easily find more useful occupation than gossiping her time away.

Vivian. I, gossip?

Fred. That's all women do when they meet!

Vivian. How awfully gallant you are today!

Fred. Then don't aggravate me with your eternal back talk!

Vivian. Do you think that a woman must always be of the same opinion as her husband?

Fred. No, of course not! But no matter what I say, you always manage to hold a different opinion! Usually, you won't even let me finish what I am saying, but interrupt me before you know— —

Vivian. [*Interrupting him.*] I never did anything like that in my life! It's impolite! Only, what's the use, when I know exactly what you are going to say?

Fred. Exactly, there you interrupt me again! You imagine you know, and answer accordingly! That's just like a woman!

Vivian. Why should you suppose that we women are absolutely devoid of any common sense? Now, I can give you a few examples——

Fred. [*Interrupting her.*] According to the latest anatomical statistics it is a proven fact that the average masculine brain weighs fully ten per cent more than the female.

Vivian. Ah, this time you interrupted me!

Fred. That has nothing to do with the question. You are merely trying to avoid it, because my argument is unanswerable.

Vivian. Fred, you are getting meaner every day! I wish I had never married! Aunt Mildred always says a woman is much happier when single.

Fred. I thought so! That old vixen is trying to poison your mind against me!

Vivian. She is at least kinder to me than you are.

[*Enter* **Torrence** C. D. *with a bundle of letters and papers in his hand.*]

Torrence. I say, Fred, are you not coming over to the office today? [*Sees* **Vivian.**] Oh, I beg your pardon. Good morning, Mrs. Parker! I understand now, he is forgetting all about the time while he is in your company.

Vivian. Good morning, Mr. Torrence. No, not exactly, I called his attention to the fact that it was after ten some time ago.

Fred. [*Irritated.*] So you did, but in what manner?

Torrence. There's no explanation needed, old fellow! I can easily understand how hard it is for a loving couple to separate, even though it be only for a few hours. [*To* **Vivian.**] Still necessity knows no law, madam, and you will excuse me if I carry off your husband, as I must consult him in regard to several important business transactions.

Vivian. Don't mention it Mr. Torrence. I am not keeping him in the least. [*Sits down again and takes up her embroidery.*]

Fred. Go ahead, Bill! I'll be at the office in less than ten minutes.

Torrence. All right. [*Aside to* **Fred.**] Not yet over the honeymoon, eh? Now don't prolong the sad and loving farewell till after lunch!

Fred. [*Sarcastically.*] There's not much danger of that!

Torrence. Good morning, Mrs. Parker. I hope you'll pardon my intrusion, but business, you know—— [*Shaking his finger at* **Fred.**] I'll give you just fifteen minutes by the clock! [*Exit laughing* C. D.]

Fred. [*Goes to table* R., *folds his newspaper together, and looks several times stealthily towards his wife. Aside.*] I would like to kiss her as usual, but it would look as if I gave into her! No. I can't afford to do it. [*Puts the newspaper under his arm and* *clears his throat.*] Hm! Hm! [*Goes up stage to* c. d. *and turns round.*]

Vivian. [*Has been nervously occupied with her embroidery, throwing repeated glances towards her husband. Aside.*] He is really going without kissing me good-bye!

Fred. [*Again clearing his throat.*] Hm! Hm!

Vivian. [*Looks at him, throws her embroidery aside, jumps up and runs towards him.*] Fred, dearest!

Fred. [*Embracing her.*] My darling! [*They come down stage together.*]

Vivian. If I hadn't looked around you would have left me without kissing me.

Fred. And if I hadn't coughed you wouldn't have looked around.

Vivian. Yes I would. I couldn't have helped myself. But we have both been acting like children, to quarrel about nothing the first thing in the morning.

Fred. Well, it's all over and forgotten now, sweetheart!

Vivian. How did it really come about?

Fred. There's no need to talk about it any more. Good bye, dear!

Vivian. No, just wait a minute! Let me think how it started!

Fred. I can't keep Torrence waiting any longer, my love!

Vivian. Now, just one second to oblige me! Let me see! Oh, yes, I remember now. I reminded you that it was past ten. That was the beginning!

Fred. The beginning wasn't the thing. The trouble was at the end. Let's start from there and then go back. You said I was getting meaner every day, and wished you had never married me!

Vivian. [*Regretfully.*] I did—but——

Fred. "But"—"but!" There really was no excuse for it! You must admit that you were wrong!

Vivian. [*Slightly provoked.*] Now, don't commence again!

Fred. [*Sighing.*] Heaven forbid!

Vivian. Previously you had said something which provoked me. Let me see! Oh, yes, you said women had no brains!

Fred. There you exaggerate again!

Vivian. [*Decisively.*] No, there's no use of you denying it. I am quite positive. [*Coaxingly.*] Come, Fred, be a good, dear little husband, and admit that it was all your fault, and that you are sorry you said so; then everything will be lovely again.

Fred. But I never said so. I can't admit what I didn't say. It wouldn't be logical!

Vivian. Whenever you are wrong you commence to throw your logic at me! I am only asking this as a favor.

Fred. But there's no sense in what you ask of me! Be reasonable, my dear. [*About to embrace her.*]

Vivian. [*Evading him*] Leave me alone. I detest you!

Fred. There you go again! Like all women! You are demanding what is impossible for me to grant, and when I try to explain——

Vivian. [*Putting her hands to her ears.*] I don't need any of your explanations!

Fred. Of course not! You're as obstinate as—as——

Vivian. Oh, go ahead! Don't mind my feelings! You meant, I am as obstinate as a mule! That's it! First you called me a vixen, and now I'm a mule!

Fred. I never called *you* a vixen, nor was it my intention to compare you to a mule. But since it amuses you to pervert everything I say——

Vivian. And I neglect my household duties, and do nothing but gossip my time away! Oh, I have a good memory!

Fred. [*Angrily.*] This is getting unbearable. [*Lifts up a chair and slams it down again.*] You would try an angel's patience!

Vivian. [*Shrinks together as if in fear.*] I won't stand this treatment. I suppose you'll be beating me next! Oh, my nerves! [*Sinks down on a chair.*]

Fred. The old story! When a woman's come to the end of her wits, she falls back on her nerves!

Vivian. [*Sobbing.*] You—you're a heartless m-m-monster!

Fred. Of course I am. I'm a monster and a tyrant. The most brutal and inhuman of all the notorious Spanish inquisitors was only a lamb compared to me! Why don't you add that I am slowly torturing you into an early grave? You might as well!

Vivian. [*Crying.*] Oh!

Mildred. [*Entering c. d.*] Good morning, children. [*Sees Vivian wiping her eyes.*] Aha! Crying, eh? [*Looking at Fred, who is excitedly walking up and down.*] Are you training for a foot-race? So, we've had another seance, eh?

Fred. It wasn't my fault.

Vivian. It certainly wasn't mine.

Fred. No,—Vivian is not feeling well. She's had an attack of the nerves!

Mildred. Indeed? So much the better!

Vivian. [*Astonished.*] Eh?

Mildred. I meant—for my purpose. I told you it was my intention to leave to-day for some watering place.

Fred. Oh, yes, I remember it quite well. [*Anxiously.*] You haven't changed your mind, have you?

Mildred. I've been putting it off constantly, because I was afraid something might happen to me!

Fred. Oh, no, impossible. Nothing could ever happen to you!

Mildred. When a lady is all alone, she's often helpless

Fred. You are old enough to take care of yourself!

Mildred. Now, last night an excellent idea struck me, and so to-day I come to ask you a great favor.

Fred. It's near the first of the month, and I am unable to help you, aunt.

Mildred. No, no, you misunderstand me!

Fred. Well, what is it then.

Mildred. Let me take Vivian with me; we won't stay away longer than a month.

Fred. [*Quickly and firmly.*] With the greatest pleasure!

Vivian. [*Rises quickly; agitated, aside.*] With the greatest pleasure!

Mildred. Did you hear, Vivian? Your husband doesn't object. Will you come with me?

Vivian. [*Restraining her emotion; quickly.*] Certainly, aunt Mildred. I'll be delighted!

Fred. [*Aside.*] Delighted, eh?

Cora. [*Entering c. d. carrying a small tray with a visiting card. To* Fred.] There's a gentleman would like to see you, sir!

Fred. To see me? Tell him to go to my office and speak to my partner.

Cora. He's just come from the office; and Mr. Torrence sent him here to see you, sir!

Fred. [*Taking the card and reading.*] "Horace D. Wallpole!" One of our customers, I think. Ask him to go to the office again. I'll meet him there in about five minutes.

Cora. Very well, sir. [*Exit c. d.*]

Mildred. [*Who has been conversing aside with* **Vivian.**] You heard it yourself, he doesn't mind your going.

Vivian. Did you say, "with the greatest pleasure," Fred?

Fred. Yes! I think aunt Mildred's plan an excellent one. You'll have a chance to recuperate your nervous system while you're away from me.

Mildred. Exactly.

Vivian. Very well then. I'll come with you, aunt, with the greatest pleasure!

Fred. [*Astonished, aside.*] Eh?

Mildred. Then it's all settled! Your household is so small that the servants will be able to look after your husband's comfort.

Fred. Oh, that's a matter of no consequence!

Vivian. Yes, only I intended to have a general housecleaning next week. [*Looks at* Fred *expectantly.*]

Mildred. The servants can do it very well, while you're away.

Vivian. There should be someone here to superintend it!

Mildred. Oh, Fred can do that!

Fred. [*Ironically.*] Oh, certainly, why not? [*Aside grumbling.*] I—superintend housecleaning!

Mildred. Well, everything is fixed now. You'd better start your packing at once. Mine is all ready!

Vivian. [*Hesitating.*] There are several other things I'll have to attend to. I can't leave Fred so suddenly, without looking after his wants first.

Mildred. Now, what's the use of making all this unnecessary fuss?

Fred. Of course, there is no use whatever. Why don't you do as your aunt tells you?

Mildred. You haven't to be fed with a spoon any more, have you?

Fred. Oh, I'll go without eating altogether, if you say so.

Mildred. You didn't starve when you were a bachelor.

Vivian. But since our marriage he is being somewhat spoiled, aunt. I have looked after all his needs and comforts, and——

Fred. Don't you worry about me, my dear. I'll eat with Torrence at some hotel or restaurant. It'll be a change at least!

Vivian. [*Looks at him reproachfully.*]

Mildred. Come, come, we're only losing time for nothing! Give me your keys, and I'll help you with your packing. We'll be able to catch the one o'clock train.

Fred. [*Ironically.*] If you should need my services, I'll——

Vivian. [*Spitefully.*] Thanks. We'll do very well without them.

Mildred. Oh, come along, Vivian! [*Exeunt* **Mildred** *and* **Vivian** L.]

Fred. [*Looking after them.*] Confound her aunt!

Torrence. [*Entering* C. D.] What's the matter, Fred? I sent that young man to you and you sent him back to the office? I've brought him back with me.

Fred. Young man? Oh, yes! [*Takes the visiting card from his vest pocket and reads.*] "Horace D. Wallpole!" Isn't that one of our customer's in Joplin, Missouri?

Torrence. Exactly. He gave this young man his card by way of introduction to us. His own name is Jones, James Jones. He wants you to do something for him.

Fred. Oh, I see! Well, Wallpole's all right, and I'll try to oblige him. [*Puts the card back in his pocket.*]

Torrence. You'd better come along. You'll have to look over the English mail, and I want to see you about several things, especially if it would be safe to extend any credit to Maclaine, Watson & Co., in Duluth.

Fred. [*Lost in thought, leaning his head on his hands; half aside.*] Only one month—four weeks! [*Sighing and somewhat louder.*] Thirty days!

Torrence. That isn't long enough!

Fred. What? Not long enough?

Torrence. They want ninety days!

Fred. Who?

Torrence. Maclaine, Watson & Co., of course!

Fred. [*Slowly.*] Oh, Maclaine, Watson & Co.

Torrence. Whom did you think I was talking about?

Fred. I was thinking of my wife.

Torrence. During your engagement to her you used often to be absent-minded. Well, then I didn't blame you, all love-sick people are more or less—— [*Pantomimic gesture expressing flight of mind.*] But now that you've been married almost two years——

Fred. [*Suddenly interrupting him.*] Bill, think of it, my wife is going away to a summer resort with her aunt for a whole month!

Torrence. Splendid idea!

Fred. What?

Torrence. I meant, if your wife is ill, it's a splendid idea for her to go there!

Fred. But she isn't ill. Never was healthier in her life. It's her aunt who is kidnapping her. That old she-dragon is in the habit of bursting in upon us like a thirteen inch shell. To-day we've had one of her explosions, and she's turned everything upside down.

Torrence. My dear fellow, now be sensible! There's no harm in a short separation! You know the old adage: "Absence makes the heart grow fonder!"

Fred. Bah, what does a confirmed bachelor like you understand of these things?

Torrence. More than you suppose! We look upon these things in a rational and sensible way, at least.

Fred. I won't be able to exist without her!

Torrence. You'll get used to it.

Fred. Never.

Torrence. You'll work a little harder, and your little wife will have a capital time!

Fred. A capital time. What do you mean? How could she have a capital time without me?

Torrence. For a married man you seem to want a considerable amount of information from a confirmed bachelor! You ought to be better posted about these things! Don't you know that there is always a lot of gay young fellows at those places?

Fred. [*Grabbing hold of* **Torrence's** *arm, excitedly.*] Gay young fellows? Are you sure? If she ever should meet any man whom she would prefer to me, I tell you I'd—— [*Shaking Torrence violently.*]

Torrence. [*Disengaging himself, laughing.*] Here, here. Don't lay violent hands on me. I'm sure it isn't my fault. [*Rubbing his arm.*] But why do you allow her to go?

Fred. I never did!

Torrence. Then all you've got to do is to ask her to stay home!

Fred. [*After reflecting a short while.*] Hm!—why, I can't do that very well. It would compromise my dignity as—as— [*Suddenly.*] Say, Will, do me a favor, have a talk with Vivian and try to persuade her not to go. Tell her I have fatty degeneration of the heart, that any shock may kill me, and that Widow's weeds won't be becoming to her particular style of beauty!

Torrence. [*Determined.*] No, Fred. I am your partner in business, but not in private matters. You must excuse me!

Fred. You might mention the subject in an off hand unconcerned way. You can easily do it, if you stay here for your lunch!

Torrence. No, thanks, old fellow. [*Declaiming.*]
    At meal time no one ever sat
    With comfort 'twixt a dog and cat!

Fred. Thanks, you're very complimentary. [*Enter* **Vivian** L. *Quickly, and aside to* Torrence.] There she is now. Go and talk to her like a good, old chap. [*Commences to whistle unconcernedly, looks at his wife, and exit* R.]

Vivian. [*Nervously and with ill-concealed anxiety.*] Mr. Torrence, what did my husband say to you?

Torrence. That he's about to become a grass-widower.

Vivian. He rather seems to like the idea of our separation.

Torrence. It should be a pleasure to him to grant your lightest wish, madam!

Vivian. But it isn't my wish at all. Aunt Mildred came, invited me to accompany her, and asked for his sanction. He said I could go "with the greatest pleasure." Just think of it! We had previously passed through a little domestic scene, that is to say, it really didn't amount to much—just as sometimes happens between the most devoted——

Torrence. [*Absent minded.*] Dog and cat. [*Quickly trying to redress himself.*] I beg your pardon, a slip of the tongue. I meant husband and wife, of course.

Vivian. Mr. Torrence, do you think my husband is rather glad at my going?

Torrence. I don't think so.

Vivian. [*Gladly.*] Really. Well, then, all he has to do is to tell me so; I'll let aunt Mildred travel alone and stay home.

Torrence. A change of air will be beneficial to you.

Vivian. I don't need any change of air. I am in excellent health.

Torrence. [*Shaking his head earnestly.*] Take my advice, Mrs. Parker, and go.

Vivian. [*Anxiously.*] What do you mean? Why should I?

Torrence. You see, when two young people get married they first live in the seventh heaven of bliss.

Vivian. Quite true, so we did.

Torrence. But this life is not all sunshine. After a while some clouds appear, even in the connubial heaven.

Vivian. So they did with us, [*Quickly,*] that is, only small ones.

Torrence. We human beings are peculiarly organized; we never

appreciate sufficiently what we fully possess. Should your husband lose your companionship for a while, he will learn to value
your presence all the more, and estimate your good qualities all
the better.

Vivian. Do you really think so?

Torrence. I am quite positive of it. You will return to him as
if for a second honeymoon, and he will again carry you on his
hands.

Vivian. [*Overjoyed.*] How lovely that would be. Yes, my
mind is made up. I'll go. It will be for his and my own happiness.

Torrence. That's right. Now you are looking at it in the
proper light.

Vivian. But I have one favor to ask of you, Mr. Torrence.
Keep a watch over him, and take good care that he behaves himself during my absence.

Torrence. Have no fear. I'll keep him so busy at the office
that he won't have time to breath, let alone to celebrate.

Vivian. And then there is one other request I have to make.
It is Fred's intention to take his meals with you at a hotel or
restaurant. I wish you would both eat here at our table. I'll
give the cook an entire menu for every day during my absence.
I know all your favorite dishes, and you will have no fault to
find.

Torrence. Very kind of you. If it is doing you a favor I'll
lunch and dine here.

Vivian. Thank you. [*Gives him her hand.*] Now, I'll go and
finish my packing with a lighter heart. [*Exit L.*]

Torrence. [*Looking after her.*] And yet to say farewell will be
a trial to the little woman. But I have done my duty.

Fred. [*Entering from R.*] Well, what did she say?

Torrence. She is going.

Fred. She is? Didn't you try to make her change her mind?

Torrence. You ought to know women better. When they've
made up their minds to do a thing there's no use to argue. Your
better half has made up her mind to accompany her aunt. That's
the end of it.

Fred. Oh, that confounded busy-body. [*Strikes his forehead
distractedly.*] Why did I speak those hasty, thoughtless words:
"with the greatest pleasure?"

Torrence. I couldn't tell you, I'm sure. One thing I do know,
she is the most considerate little wife I ever met. You have no
idea how anxious she is about your welfare during her trip. But
here, I am talking my time away while that young man is waiting.
Will you see him here or come back with us to the office?

Fred. I can't come just yet. I will have to get some money
ready for her first.

Torrence. Then I'd better send that young fellow up here?

Fred. Just as you like. I suppose he's in need of some financial aid.

Torrence. Probably. And what about Maclaine, Watson & Co? Shall we give them ninety days credit?

Fred. Ninety years, for all I care. [*Exit dejectedly* R.]

Torrence. Now, there's an up-to-date business man for you.

Cora. [*Enters* C. D. *followed by* **Hebe.**] Please, step in this room, Miss. I will call the lady. [*Exit* L.]

Hebe. I was told at her appartments that I should find Miss Green here. Have I the pleasure to see Mr. Parker?

Torrence. I beg your pardon, Miss. I am his partner. Won't you please take a chair?

Hebe. Thank you, sir. [*Sits down.*]

Torrence. Miss Green will be here directly, I presume. Will you kindly excuse me? [*Exit* C. D. *after bowing.*]

Cora. [*Enters* L.] Miss Green asks if you will kindly wait a few minutes; she is busy packing a trunk.

Hebe. Certainly. Thank you.

Cora. [*Goes up stage to* C. D. *and meets* **James Jones,** *who enters.*]

Jones. [*To Cora.*] Mr. Parker's partner told me I would find him up here.

Cora. Please step in, sir. He'll be here directly. [*Exit* C. D.]

Jones. [*Sees* **Hebe.**] Ah! [*Bows.*] Have I the pleasure to see Mrs. Parker?

Hebe. [*Rises.*] No, sir. I am only a stranger here, and waiting to see Miss Green, Mrs. Parker's aunt.

Jones. Then I hope you'll be more successful on your errand than I have been on mine. I want to see Mr. Parker. I went to his office this morning, his partner sends me here, he sends me back to his partner at the office, his partner takes me back from the office, and brings me here, saying I'll find him here. But I don't find him here. I wonder where he is?

Hebe. I'm sure I'm unable to tell you, sir.

Jones. Of course you are, since you are also a stranger here. But, please, be seated again.

Hebe. [*Sits down again.*]

Jones. [*Aside.*] Charming young lady. [*Aloud.*] Will you allow me to assist you in waiting, Miss?

Hebe. Certainly, sir.

Jones. [*After a short pause.*] It's so much nicer to wait in company.

Hebe. Yes, sir. [*Short pause.*]

Jones. In this life everything is born easier when it is shared, happiness as well as sorrow.

Hebe. Yes, sir.

Jones. [*After a short pause.*] Do you live here in Chicago, madam.

Hebe. Yes, sir.

Jones. It seems rather a dusty and smoky place. Must be a good town for the laundry business. Still, I shall be glad to remain here for a while.

Hebe. And I am glad to get away from here for some time.

Jones. Are you going to leave here? I'm sorry to hear it.

Hebe. I've come here to ask Miss Green, who leaves to-day, to keep rooms at her hotel reserved for us.

Jones. May I ask where you are going?

Hebe. We are going to a summer resort I go as companion and nurse of an invalid, old uncle of mine.

Jones. That must be a rather tiresome job.

Hebe. Oh, no, sir, not at all I owe everything to my uncle, and to do one's duty should never be tiresome.

Jones. So dutiful, and yet so young, madam.

Hebe. Should youth be a barrier to the performance of one's duty?

Jones. [*Enthusiastically.*] At last I have found the white raven I have been looking for; a young lady with principles.

Hebe. You are making fun of me, sir.

Jones. Not at all, madam, I never was more serious in all my life. Now-a-days most young ladies are superficial, all they think of are their dresses and their amusements.

Hebe. What of the young gentlemen, though? Are they all perfection? Most of them are flirts, and weary us with their stale compliments.

Jones. Luckily there are exceptions.

Hebe. I have never met them.

Jones. [*Confused.*] Indeed? [*Short pause.*] It seems they have forgotten all about us. [*Picks up a book.*]

Hebe. You must be getting tired of waiting. Don't let me prevent you from reading, sir.

Jones. I beg your pardon. I merely picked up this book by accident. I did not mean to be rude. [*Aside.*] She has some spirit, too. She's simply adorable.

Mildred. [*Entering* L.] You wish to see me, madam, I am Miss Green.

Hebe. [*Rises.*] My name is Hebe Worthy.

Jones. [*Rises, aside.*] Hebe! Lovely name.

Hebe. Your physician happens to be the same one who is treating my uncle, and on account of this I have called on you to request a favor.

Mildred. [*Pointing at* Jones.] And this gentleman?

Hebe. We are strangers, madam

Jones. [*Bowing.*] Yes, unfortunately. We were just beginning to get better acquainted when you interrupted us. My name is Jones. I am waiting to see Mr. Parker.

Mildred. Oh. [*To* Hebe.] Will you, please, follow me? [*Goes to door* L. *followed by* Hebe.]

Jones. [*About to follow them.*] With pleasure.

Mildred. [*Haughtily.*] I did not mean you, sir. You'll probably find Mr. Parker at his office.

Jones. Pardon me, madam, but I've been there already twice this morning.

Mildred. Then you had better wait for him here. [*Opens door L.; to Hebe.*] If you please. [*Hebe exit L. followed by Mildred.*]

Jones. [*Bowing.*] Good day, ladies!——— She's gone. Hebe! Adorable creature. An angel, a fairy; with principles. I must meet her again. She is going to a summer resort. But she didn't mention to which one. [*Sees Parker, who enters room. Inquiringly.*] Mr. Parker, I presume?

Fred. Yes, sir. You want to see me?

Jones. Mr. Torrence advised me to wait for you here.

Fred. Oh, I see. You are the young man introduced to us by Mr. Wallpole, of Joplin?

Jones. Yes, sir. I am a distant relative of his, and being a total stranger in Chicago, he took the liberty to give me a sort of introduction to you. He said he would write to you in a few days.

Fred. It will be a pleasure to me to oblige any relative of so old a business acquaintance as Mr. Wallpole. Unfortunately I am extremely busy just now, so if you will kindly state the amount——— [*Takes out his pocketbook.*]

Jones. [*Perplexed.*] Mr. Parker, I think you———

Fred. [*Interrupting him.*] Come, don't be bashful! I'll square things again with Wallpole.

Jones. Pardon me, Mr. Parker, but you seem to labor under some mistake. I haven't come to you for any financial aid. Do I appear to you like a beggar?

Fred. [*Somewhat confused.*] Not at all, my dear sir. You really must excuse me. I meant no offence. My head is so full of other things, you see. My wife, for instance, is going away with her aunt to-day, and———

Jones. [*Interrupting him; eagerly.*] May I ask to which place she is going?

Fred. Really, I haven't heard her mention the name, and it doesn't matter. But, excuse me, take a seat, please. Now tell me what can I do for you?

Jones. I have come to Chicago with the ultimate intention of starting in business for myself. But in order to get located and acquainted, I would first like to find a position as clerk, correspondent or bookkeeper with some well established firm. I have had considerable experience in smaller towns, and the matter of salary is of a secondary consideration.

Fred. So, you're looking for a position? In our line of business? Dry goods?

Jones. No, sir! Drugs!

Fred. That's fortunate. My brother-in-law, Owens, is head of the firm Owens, Kirk & Co., wholesale druggists on Randophl street. I met him yesterday, and he told me he was looking for an experienced bookkeeper, who had some knowledge of drugs.

Jones. [*Sees a rosebud lying on the stage.*] Ah, a rosebud! [*Picks it up.*] Some one must have dropped it. Just now I met a charming young lady here who——

Fred. [*Taking the rosebud from Jones' hand.*] Very much obliged! [*Lays rosebud on table.*] Now, I will give you my card. Here it is. I'll write the firm's name and address on the back of it. [*Writes on card and hands it to Jones.*] Insist on seeing Mr. Owens himself, tell him I sent you, and hand him my card. Explain to him that I would have written him a note, but that I am very busy just now, on account of my wife going on a trip. I have no doubt but that you will suit my brother-in-law, and that you will make satisfactory terms with him.

Jones. Thank you, Mr. Parker. I am in no particular hurry though. Before accepting a position, I intended to take a month's holiday, as I have been constantly employed for the last three years, and I thought a little travelling would do me good. May I ask whether the ladies intend to go east or south?

Fred. [*Suspiciously.*] How can this possibly concern, you, sir?

Jones. You see, it doesn't matter to me which way I go, and perhaps I might be of service to them They could travel under my care and protection.

Fred. [*Looks at him in utter amazement.*]

Jones. [*After a short pause.*] I mean, that ladies who travel alone, often need some assistance, and——

Fred. [*Interrupting him; frigidly.*] Let me advise you to mind your own business, Mr. ——, I really do not remember your name.

Jones. Jones, sir. Plain Jim Jones.

Fred. Then allow me to wish you good day, Mr. Jones. [*Goes towards* R. *Aside.*] This beats anything in the way of plain American gall I have ever met. [*Exit* R.]

Jones. [*Politely.*] Allow me once more to thank you, Mr. Parker. [*Alone.*] I don't care a rap where his ladies go to, but I must know how I can get on the track of my little Hebe! How to find out? Ah, I'll leave my gloves here. When I come back for them, somebody will surely give me the necessary information. [*Takes off his gloves and places them on table* R.] It's an old dodge, but it always works. [*Goes up stage towards* C. D. *Enters* Cora C. D. *Aside.*] Ah, my saviour. The walking encyclopædia of domestic information. [*To Cora.*] I say, my dear, is Mrs. Parker very ill?

Cora. Not that I know, sir!

Jones. But she's going away to some summer resort?

Cora. Rich people go there to have fun, not for their health!

Jones. To which place is she going?

Cora. I couldn't tell you sir.

Jones. You surely must have heard her mention the name. Just try and remember!

Cora. I only heard of her going this morning, sir, and I'm certain I don't know where she is going.

Jones. But you'll be able to find out. I am very anxious to know! Here, let me sharpen your seemingly extreme dullness of perception and memory, [Gives her a banknote.] Now, get me the information I am looking for!

Cora. Thank you, sir!—I will.

Jones. I suppose you don't mind my taking this flower, do you? [Takes the rosebud from the table.]

Cora. Not at all, sir!

Jones. I'll call again after a short while, and if you can tell me the name of that place, [taps on the money in his pocket] your reward will be in due accordance with my appreciation and gratitude. [Pats her on the cheek. Sees Fred coming from R.] I'll see you later on! [Exit quickly C. D.]

Fred. [Entering from R.] Who was that, Cora?

Cora. [Confused.] Nobody, sir,—— that is, only the young gentleman who called on you, sir! He took a rosebud from the table! That's all, sir!

Fred. [Annoyed.] What? He had the impudence?

Cora. It was all withered anyhow, sir!

Fred. [Angrily.] What else did he want of you?

Cora. [Frightened.] N-n-nothing much, sir!

Fred. Come, come, no nonsense! Out with it!

Cora. He only wanted to know what place Mrs. Parker was going to!

Fred. Did you tell him?

Cora. No, sir. I don't know it myself. [Aside.] I wonder what's come over them all to-day! [Exit L.]

Fred. It's beyond my comprehension! He can only have seen my wife for a single moment, and falls head over heels in love with her. The trouble is, she's too attractive! That's what they'll all find out at that confounded resort. They'll be paying compliments to her, and flattering her, and heaven knows, trying to flirt with her. It makes my blood boil when I think of it. [Walks up and down in great excitement.]

Torrence. [Enters C. D.] Well, I've closed that deal with Maclaine, Watson & Co!

Fred. [Without paying attention to him, still moving about.] It won't do! It won't do!

Torrence. But you gave your sanction in the matter!

Fred. I was too hasty,—— yes, it's pure nonsense!

Torrence. It's an old and solid firm.

Fred. [Stops walking.] Solid firm. What firm?

Torrence. Maclaine, Watson & Co., of course.

Fred. Ah, I'm talking of my wife!

Torrence. [*Drops into a chair in disgust.*] Great Scott, what a business man!

Fred. [*Resuming his walking; aside.*] He must have known her previously, otherwise it's impossible. I must make sure of this. [*Suddenly stopping in front of* **Torrence.**] Will, I am going to follow my wife tomorrow.

Torrence. Are you going to make a laughing stock of yourself?

Fred. No, sir. I have an idea. I'll go there disguised, so nobody will know me. I'll be watching her without being recognized. Do you understand me?

Torrence. [*Firmly.*] I do not. [*Aside.*] He's going daffy!

Fred. It's all quite simple. I'll shave off my beard, dye my hair, put on a new suit of clothes, assume a false name, and there you are. Not a soul—not even my wife—will know me. I'll be there to protect her from insults, to shield her from impudence and annoyance. No fresh dude shall come within ten feet of her.

Torrence. You'll have your hands full with those feet.

Fred. Don't try to be funny! This is serious, most serious. I will leave you a bunch of letters to her, which your will mail as if they came from me. That will make the deception complete.

Torrence. And what about our business?

Fred. It's safe in your hands. Some future day, when you are married I'll be able to repay you.

Torrence. Heaven forbid! The example you are setting me is not at all enticing.

Fred. Before I forget it, I must telephone to Owens and tell him to throw that loafer Jones out of his office when he calls. [*Exit* R.]

Mildred. [*Enters from* L. *followed by* **Hebe.**] You may count on me, Miss Worthy, everything will be ready for your uncle when he arrives.

Hebe. This is so kind of you, Miss Green. I hope you will pardon my presumptuous request, but my uncle insisted on my calling on you, and his illness makes him so irritable, that I was compelled to consent.

Mildred. Don't mention it, my dear! You tell your uncle that he will find his rooms engaged, and in order when he gets there! [*Shakes hands with her.*] I won't say good-bye as we will meet again in a couple of days.

Hebe. Good-bye, Miss Green, till then—and allow me to thank you once more. [*Bows to* Torrence *and exit* C. D.]

Mildred. I cannot understand my niece at all any more, Mr. Torrence. She is going on a pleasure trip, and instead of feeling glad at the prospect, all she does is sighing, Sniffing and wiping her eyes. She is packing her trunk, and I'm afraid all her clothes will be damp, the way she goes on.

Torrence. Yes, and Fred is tearing out his hair, and behaving himself like a lunatic in general.

Mildred. Well, you'll be here to console him.

Torrence. I'll do the best I can, but I'm afraid it's a hopeless case. But excuse me, I'll have to go back to the office. Allow me to wish you a pleasant trip! [*They shake hands.*]

Mildred. Thank you, Mr. Torrence, and good bye!—[*Exit* Torrence c. d. *Enter* Vivian l., *followed by* Cora, *who drags on a wicker basket, which she places up stage* c., *in front of* c. d.] So I'm glad to see you are ready at last. [Cora *exit* l., *and returns later on with hand-satchels, shawls and umbrellas, which she places on top of the basket.* Vivian *is furtively wiping her eyes.*] Now, Vivian, do have a little sense. Don't let Fred see what it costs you to leave him for a short while. Otherwise he'll think that you can't exist without him.

Vivian. [*Wiping her eyes.*] Neither can I!

Mildred. You only imagine so. A sensible woman should never show her weakness, or else she's lost. This short separation will lead to your ultimate happiness.

Vivian. I know. Mr. Torrence told me the same thing. [*With determination.*] Yes, I must. I will be strong. [*Resolutely wipes her eyes and puts away her handkerchief.*] I've made up my mind. There!—[*Sees* Fred *who enters* r., *and commences to hum some popular air, in which she is joined by* Mildred *who sings out of tune.*]

Fred. [*Remains near door* r., *astonished. Aside.*] She has the heart to sing at a time like this. [*Aloud.*] Well, I see you have finished your packing.

Vivian. Yes, everything is quite ready.

Fred. You seem to be in a dreadful hurry to leave, my dear.

Mildred. [*Goes to* Fred *and takes him aside in* r. *corner.*] My dear Fred, don't make this leave taking more painful than you can help, or else your wife will think you are unable to live without her.

Fred. No more can I.

Mildred. Pure imagination! A man of common sense doesn't carry his heart on his sleeve. If he does, he's bound to be henpecked.

Fred. I'll be master of my feelings all right!—I swear it! [*Lifts up his hand.*]

Mildred. [*Pulls down his hand.*] Don't!—We old maids don't take stock in masculine oaths. [*To* Vivian.] Now, I'll run over home, Vivy, and get ready myself. I'll be back directly. Please, don't quarrel again, while I am gone. [*Exit* c. d]

Vivian. Fred, how often do you want to hear from me?

Fred. It's rather difficult to lay down rules in a question of that kind, but I should think as often as your own heart dictates you to write.

Vivian. [*Forgetting herself and affectionately.*] Oh, then, I'll write you at least twice every d— [*Recollecting herself.*] Every week.

Fred. [*Coolly.*] I guess that will do.

Vivian. The way you talk—it seems to be a matter of absolute indifference to you. I commence to believe that it is somewhat of a relief to you, to be rid of me for some time.

Fred. And I think it's the other way. I have never yet seen any one who seemed so anxious to finish packing and be gone.

Vivian. Oh, that's aunt Mildred's doing. She hurried me so. But if you want me to, I'll tell her that we won't leave till to-morrow!

Fred. [*Mastering himself.*] Oh, no, not at all! When once you've made up your mind, it's always better to stick to the original plan. I'll get some body to carry your things down. [*Goes towards* c. D.]

Vivian. Fred!

Fred. [*Turning round.*] Well?

Vivian. You'll write often, won't you?

Fred. Oh, yes every—— [*Correcting himself.*] Twice every week. [*Exit* c. D.]

Vivian. [*Sadly.*] Well, I think I've kept it up bravely!

Cora. [*Who has entered previously, and has been arranging the different objects on top of the wicker basket.*] Do you intend to stay away long, ma'am?

Vivian. Yes, Cora—four weeks.

Cora. Then I hope Mr. Parker won't act like he did before.

Vivian. [*Frightened.*] What do you mean Cora? When?

Cora. When you went to visit your sick mother, and stayed away for two days. The master never touched a bite during the whole time. He said he had no appetite and couldn't eat without you!

Vivian. [*Gladly.*] Really! Did he say that?

Cora. If he's going to keep this up for four weeks he'll be turned into a skeleton, I'm afraid.

Vivian. Mr. Torrence is going to take his meals here while I'm away, so my husband will have company and won't feel so lonesome. Please, get your slate and write down the bill of fare for the rest of this week!

Cora. Yes ma'am. [*Exit* L.]

Vivian. [*Sadly.*] Poor fellow! He couldn't eat without me! And see how I am treating him now. Oh, I am a bad, undutiful wife!—I deserve it that he sends me away from him.

Cora. [*Enters* L. *with a slate, to which is attached a small sponge and a slate pencil. On entering she is cleaning the slate with the sponge.*] All right ma'am!—I'm ready!

Vivian. [*Aside.*] This has taken all my courage from me! [*Aloud.*] Well, for to-morrow, pea soup—he likes it rather thick!

Cora. [*Writing on the slate.*] Yes, ma'am!

Vivian. Baked white fish, with butter sauce. French fried potatoes.

Cora. [*Same bus.*] Yes, ma'am.

Vivian. Veal cutlets, breaded, with— [*Gulping down a sob.*]—ato sauce! [*Begins softly to cry.*]

Cora. What kind of sauce ma'am?

Vivian. Tomato sauce! [*Wipes her eyes.*]

Cora. [*Sees that* **Vivian** *is weeping, also tearfully.*] Oh, ma'am, what's the use of your leaving us?

Vivian. [*Trying to restrain her tears.*] Give me the slate, I'll write it down myself! [*Takes the slate from* **Cora.**] Please leave me alone now!

Cora. [*Weeping and drying her tears with the corners of her apron. Aside.*] I'm that soft-hearted I can't bear to see the Missus crying without wanting to keep her company. [*Bursts out sobbing.*]

Mildred. [*Enters* c. d. *with travelling hat, linen duster, large satchel, several bundles, boxess, packages, large umbrella, birdcage, etc., and followed by* **Jones.**] This way, sir!

Vivian. [*Rising, startled.*] A stranger?

Mildred. This gentleman left his gloves here!

Jones. Yes!—I beg a thousand pardons for the intrusion. Very stupid of me, of course. [*Searches for his gloves.*] Ah, there they are! [*Picks them up from table* R.]

Mildred. [*Aside to* **Vivian.**] I'm ashamed of you Vivian! How can you be so weak?

Jones. [*Aside to* **Cora.**] Well, what's the name of the place?

Cora. *Wiping her eyes.*] Oh, don't bother me!—I don't know! [*Turns away from him.*[

Jones. Then there's only one thing left for me to do. I'll wait down stairs and follow the ladies to the depot.

Fred. [*Enters* c. d. *sees* **Jones,** *and goes towards him in a threatening manner.*] Now, what in the devil's name are you doing here again?

Jones. I'm sure, I beg your pardon! [*Shows the gloves, which he is putting on.*] I came for my gloves, which I accidentally left here this morning.

Fred. Indeed? Have you called on Owens yet?

Jones. No, sir, not yet!

Fred. Then you'd better hurry. I telephoned him about you, and he's waiting for you!

Jones. Very kind of you, I'm sure!

Fred. [*Angrily pushing* **Jones** *up stage towards* c. d.] Hurry up!—Don't keep him waiting!

Jones. [*Lifting up one side of the basket.*] Can I perhaps assist you in taking this basket down?

Fred. [*Lifting up the other side of the basket and pushing* **Jones,** *who retains hold of it, off the stage.*] No, sir!

Jones. [*Off stage.*] A pleasant trip, ladies! [*During preced-*

ing dialogue **Mildred** *has assisted* **Vivian** *in putting on her hat and cloak.* **Fred** *is up stage behind the basket, which remains in view of the audience.* **Vivian** *runs towards him. They embrace each other across the basket.*]

   *Vivian. [*Tearfully.*] Good bye, dearest Fred!

   *Fred. [*Sadly.*] Good bye, my darling!

   *Mildred. [*Pulling* **Vivian** *by the arm.*] Come along! Enough of this!

   *Cora. [*Bursting out in tears.*] This breaks my heart!

   [**Rapidly.*]

Picture—Quick Curtain.

<h1 align="center">ACT II.</h1>

   Scene: *Lawn in front of the Park Hotel in Waukesha. Hotel with veranda and steps* L. *Down stage* L. *an arbor with striped awnings over it. Small tables and garden chairs* R. *Garden drop. Wood wings and foliage borders.* **Otto** *discovered arranging a breakfast on table in arbor* L. *Enter* **Police Sergeant Ripley** R.

   Sergeant. Good morning, Otto!

   Otto. [*Speaking with strong German accent.*] Ach, good morning, sergeant! It's a loffely morning already, don't it? [*Continues setting the table.*]

   Sergeant. How is things? Many guests arrived since yesterday?

   Otto. Oh, just so, so! Not so many as that! They don't come as vot dey used to so quick. Years ago dey come already one month before now! Und the waiter business ist ausgespielt, I bet you some!

   Sergeant. I suppose you don't get as many tips as you used to, eh?

   Otto. Ach vot! Noddings like it! I joost as well work in a beergarden in Meelvaukee, I dell you. When there is not peoples enough here, how can you oxpect to make tips? Und ven dey come, de gendelmans is so stingy as de teufel. Und de ladies are more vorse as de gentlemans yet.

Sergeant. Well, Otto, I tell you what you might do, if you don't want to be a waiter any more,—you'd better join the force!

Otto. Me be a policeman, Sergeant? No, sir, thank you! Not so long as I vos strong enough to work, I bet you some.

Sergeant. [*Going towards hotel* L.] Ha-ha-ha! Good for you, dutchy. But I think I'll have a peep at the register, we're looking for a swell "con" from New York. He might be among last night's arrivals. [*Exit in hotel* L.]

Otto. Ach, vot, De policemens here never catch anydings already yet. Dey couldn't even catch de momps, of dey tried, I bet you. [**Dr. Rogers** *enters* R. U. E. *and goes towards hotel, when* **Otto** *sees him.*] Och, doctor, doctor!

Dr. Rogers. Well, Otto, what is it?

Otto. Dere's an old gentleman vot come last night in 53, und he vants you badly, I bet you.

Dr. Rogers. What seems to be the matter with him?

Otto. I dunno, doctor, but I think it was a complicashun of all de diseases in the alphabet. A little consumpshun, some skeeatica, some lumbago, a little epiglottis und epizootic, und a bit of cholera morpus und minagitis, just to keep dings going. He vos ringing his bell every five minutes for hot water, cold water, icewater, Hunyade water, Silurian spring water, quinine pills, porous plasters, mustard foot-baths und all sorts of dings. He's tired out six bell boys since he come, und dey'll all go on a strike, of he keeps it up. He has asked after you about a dozen times already yet, doctor.

Dr. Rogers. What's his name?

Otto. Mr. Gr-r-rowler!

Dr. Rogers. What's his business, do you know?

Otto. Och, I dink nothing at all. More likely only just to be sick! Dot seems to keep him pretty busy!

Dr. Rogers. Well—if he'll only follow my instructions faithfully, I guess our climate and water will put him on his feet again.

Otto. Yes, doctor—dis climate is very healthy for de feet!—Will you go up now already, und see him?

Dr. Rogers. [*Looking at his watch.*] No, I'll have to go across to the park for a moment, but I'll be back in about ten minutes. You can tell Mr. Growler I'll see him then. [*Exit* R. U. E.]

Otto. All right, doctor!—Now, dere's a man vot makes his money easy, I bet you some!—Och, of I vos a doctor I vouldn't be a waiter!

[*Enter* **Growler** *and* **Hebe** *from hotel* L.]

Hebe. See, uncle, how pretty it is out here!—And what a lovely place to take our breakfast!

Growler. [*A large shawl over his shoulders, grumbling.*] Hm, may be!—There's plenty of air here, at least!—Inside it's stiffling enough to be smothered!—Of course they had to put us over the dining room!—And then they have the pretention to call this a first-class hotel!—Bah!

Otto. [*Making himself very officious.*] Good morning, sir!— Good morning madam! Was dere anythings I could already do for you?

Growler. [*Not paying any attention to him.*] Then the smell of cooking in my bedroom!—It's very unhealthy!—I'm afraid I'll get worse instead of better here!—And the rooms are so infernally small!—Besides I never heard such a confounded continual racket as is going on in this place!—I couldn't sleep a wink all night!— And this morning between the clattering of dishes below and the hollering of chambermaids and children in the halls, it was enough to set one crazy!—Bah!

Otto. Ah, Mr. Growler, but dere's a very fine view from your windows!

Growler. [*Turning angrily towards him.*] Fine view, sir?— Fine view?—Will that give me back my health?—Will it, sir?—I came here for pure air, and plenty of it—and rest—and quiet!— That's what I'm paying for, sir!—Do I get it, eh?—Answer me that, sir!—Bah!

Hebe. [*Trying to pacify him.*] Now, uncle, don't excite yourself!—You know it's bad for you!—Where would you like to have our breakfast served?

Growler. Wherever there is no draught, of course! [*Pointing to arbor* L.] That seems a fairly suitable place over there!—Bring us our breakfast, waiter, quick!—I've left the order with the clerk. —Hurry up!—[*Goes towards* L.]

Otto. Yes, sir!—But excuse me, sir, would you please take some other table!—Dat one vos reserved for Miss Green of No. 34! [*Exit quickly in hotel* L.]

Growler. Reserved?—Are the seats reserved here like in a theatre?—Bah, nonsense!—I'll sit here and nowhere else!—First come, first served. [*Sits down at table in arbor* L.] Here I am, and here I'll stay!

Hebe. Maybe Miss Green will not object to our company.— That's the lady, uncle, who was so kind as to order our rooms ahead for us.

Growler. [*Jumping up.*] The devil!—I don't want to meet her!—Let's get away from here as far as we can! [*Grumbling.*] Of course, she had to choose the only place that's somewhat protected!—Bah! [*Goes towards* R.]

Hebe. [*Following him.*] There are plenty of other nice places, uncle.

Growler. But they're not covered!—Suppose it should commence to rain? [*Sits down* R.]

Hebe. There's not a cloud in the sky, uncle, and it's not at all likely that it will rain!

Growler. Yes—I know these summer resorts!—It's always the

unexpected that happens! [*Bringing his hands to his head.*]
There's a draught here!—Did you bring my muffler?

Hebe. Yes—here it is, uncle! [*Gives him a large muffler.*] I
can't feel a breath of air.

Growler. [*Winding the muffler round his neck.*] Of course
not.—Your senses are not as finely developed as mine!—Unless
her hat blows off a woman never feels a draught!

Otto. [*Entering from hotel* L.] Ah, you vish to sit here?—All
right, sir! [*Spreads a white tablecloth over table in front of*
Growler.] You will find this also a very loffely place, sir.—I bet
you!

Growler. My feet are getting cold!—[*Feels the ground with
his hand.*] I think the ground is damp!

Otto. Oh, no, sir!—It's as dry as anydings!

Growler. Nonsense!—Bah!—It's, of course, full of spring
moisture and dew!—I might as well sit in a marsh! [*Places his
feet on one of the rungs of his chair.*]

Hebe. Wait a minute, uncle!—I'll get you a footstool! [*Exit
in hotel* L.]

Otto. I never heerd anyone gomplain of damp here before, sir,
—I bet you some! [*Keeps on spreading the tablecloth, taking it
up, shaking it, turning it, and pulling it straight, etc.*

Growler. Because they were a lot of fools!—[*Grabbing his
head again.*] This draught is something terrible! [*Suddenly and
angrily.*] Say,—will you stop monkeying with that confounded
tablecloth! It makes me nervous!

Otto. Oh, yes, sir!—All right, sir!

Hebe. [*Entering from hotel* L. *with footstool.*] Here you are,
uncle!— [*Places footstool under his feet.*]

Growler. [*Somewhat kinder.*] Thank you, my dear! [*To* **Otto.**]
Bring me a cover for my knees!

Otto. Yes, sir! All right, sir. [*Exit in hotel* L.]

Hebe. You don't seem to be in good humor to-day, uncle.
But after we get acquainted with some of the other guests here,
you'll have more distraction.

Growler. I don't care for any distraction, and I don't wish to
get acquainted with anyone here!—You'll oblige me, Hebe, by
forming no acquaintances whatever while here,—do you understand? Absolutely none!

Hebe. Very well, uncle,—but it would seem very impolite if we
didn't thank the ladies who ordered our rooms for us.

Growler. You can attend to that,—I don't want to meet them.
—If I did I would probably have to dance attendance upon them,
and carry their shawls, parasols, fans or such things!— If it should
rain, they would use my umbrella, and leave me to get wet!—No,
I know all about those things!—Is that waiter never coming back
with a rug?—I'm almost freezing!

Hebe. [*Rises.*] I'll go after it, uncle.

Growler. No,—never mind! [*Rises.*] I'll take a little exercise,

—I'm getting stiff sitting here!—How can anyone possibly expect to get his health in a hole like this! [*Exit grumbling* R. U. E.]

Hebe. [*Sadly.*] This is rather a gloomy prospect,—not to be allowed to speak to any one!

Otto. [*Entering from hotel* L.] Here vos de cover already!

Hebe. Put it on this chair!—My uncle will be back directly! [*Goes up stage.*]

Otto. All right, madam.—I will bring your breakfast now! [*Goes towards* L. *and is met by* **Jones,** *who comes from the hotel.*]

Jones. Say, waiter,—I am expecting an elderly, sickly gentleman, attended by a young lady;— let me know immediately when they arrive!

Otto. They have arrived last night already, sir!

Jones. Where can I find them?

Otto. The old gentleman is gone for a valk, I dink,—und the young lady is dere! [*Points over his shoulder with his thumb towards* **Hebe.**]

Jones. By jove,—so she is!—All right Hans,—scoot!

Otto. Oxcuse me, sir,—but my name vos not Hans Scoot,—it vos Otto! [*Exit in a mock dignified manner in hotel* L.]

Jones. [*Approaching* **Hebe** *who has been looking off stage, and has not seen him.*] Allow me to wish you a good morning, miss!

Hebe. [*Turns round, astonished, bowing.*] Good morning, sir!

Jones. You probably do not remember me?

Hebe. Oh, yes, sir,—your names is Jones! —I am surprised to see you here!

Jones. Yes,——so am I!

Hebe. Are you here for your health?

Jones. No,—not exactly!——Will you permit me to tell you what brought me here?

Hebe. If you like!

Jones. I am here,—because I wished to follow you!

Hebe. [*Astonished.*] Follow me, sir!

Jones. Exactly!—I wanted to meet you again!—Probably you'll call my conduct impudent and obtrusive,— I can not help it! —— I hope at least that you will believe me sincere!

Hebe. I do not understand you, sir!

Jones. Nor do I understand it myself!—Nobody could possibly find it more incomprehensible than I do!—Although I tried every means in my power to discover day before yesterday which particular watering place you were going to visit, I was unsuccessful, and all I could do was to follow Mrs. Parker and her aunt.—The aunt bought the tickets,—I stood behind her, but could not hear what destination she got them for,—so after she had finished, I stepped up to the ticket-window and asked for a ticket to the same place! I got it, and found that they were going to Waukesha!—I stepped on board the train after them,—and here I am, without any baggage—not even a satchel,—and, as I had barely money enough in my pocket at the time for my ticket,—without money!—What do you think of it?

Hebe. I think, sir, that you have acted very foolishly!

Jones. Exactly my opinion!—Still the saying goes that it is always a wise plan to follow one's first impulse!

Hebe. That's what somnambulists do, and yet many of them make a misstep and are dashed to pieces!

Jones. [*Beseechingly.*] Ah,—but you will not allow me to be dashed, will you?—Besides, I am fully awake,—the sun shines brightly,—and I see you standing before me!—It is no dream, but sweet reality!—I am sure that I am here to find my life's happiness!

Hebe. Mr. Jones,—you must think me very innocent, if you believe that all this talk makes any impression on me!

Jones. I believe you to be a most sensible little lady. Just think of it,—I really do not even know whether you are a blonde or a brunette!

Hebe. I am sorry that your eyesight is so bad!

Jones. I do not know whether you are eighteen or forty years old!

Hebe. Thanks!—You are very complimentary!

Jones. All I know is that you are different from other women, that you are exercising an irresistible influence over me!—And it is exactly because I take you to be so sensible, that I am telling you all this!

Hebe. [*Sarcastically.*] That's very kind of you!—But will you please inform me what your purpose is with all these flattering comments!

Jones. They are no flatteries,—I am merely stating facts!—My purpose is that you should be aware of them, and my only hope —that you should wish to know me better!—That is all!—But in the first place, it is necessary that I should make your uncle's acquaintance!—I would consider it a favor if you will give me an introduction to him!

Hebe. I am sorry, but that is absolutely impossible!—He has positively forbidden me to make him acquainted with any of the other guests! The state of his health has made him very irritable, and I cannot act contrary to his wishes.

Jones. I wouldn't like you to incur his displeasure for anything in the world!—I'll introduce myself to him!

Hebe. You will find it no easy matter!

Jones. When I've made up my mind to do a thing, I generally succeed!—I am somewhat of a student of human nature, and know that everybody has some weak point.—Can you tell me what is you uncle's favorite topic?

Hebe. He prefers to talk about his health and the different cures he is taking.

Jones. Splendid subject of conversation! I suppose everybody here talks about it!—I will succeed,—I am sure!

Hebe. Only do not let him suspect that we are acquainted!—
There he comes from the Park now!

Jones. But you do not mind my introducing myself? [*Hebe
shakes her head.*] That's enough!—Thanks! [*Hebe goes to meet
Growler and exit R. U. E.*]

Otto. [*Enters with breakfast tray from hotel L. To Jones.*]
The clerk vants to kuow of he shall send for your trunk from the
depot, sir!

Jones. No,—I came without baggage!

Otto. Oh, you don't come for your health, sir? Only tr-rans-
ient, eh?

Jones. Not exactly,—I intend to stay here for some time!—My
baggage will come later on!

Otto. [*Looking at him suspiciously.*] Ach, so! [*Aside.*] No
trunk and no satchel, eh?—I'll have to tell the clerk!—[*Places the
breakfast on table R.—Jones exits in hotel L.—Enter Growler
and Hebe R. U. E.*]

Growler. Hebe, I believe the air here is doing me good!—My
head seems clearer, and I've had an excellent idea!

Hebe. Really, uncle!—I'm so glad!—And what is the idea?

Otto. Your br-reakfast is ready, sir!

Growler. [*Brusquely.*] Do you think I'm blind?—You needn't
wait!

Otto. [*Feeling himself insulted, aside.*] Dot sour-faced hyena!
—I'll get even with him, I bet you some! [*Exit in hotel L. with
mock dignity.*]

Growler. [*Mysteriously.*] I've discovered a way to find out
what is really the matter with me! [*They sit down at table R. and
commence to eat.*]

Hebe. Oh, uncle, dear,—that would be such a relief!

Growler. [*Taking a letter from his pocket.*] Look at this!—
It's a letter written by my doctor in Chicago to Dr. Rogers of the
sanitorium here in regard to the state of my health and his treatment of me.—Doctors will never tell their patients what their ailments are, but they'll discuss the matter with each other, of
course.—All I'll have to do is to open this letter, and find the
information I want!

Hebe. But, uncle,—you surely wouldn't do this?

Growler. And why not?

Hebe. I think you had better not.

Growler. You see,—you are afraid to know the worst!—But I
prefer to know it rather than be left in all this uncertainty!—I
may never have a chance like this again!—I'll have a cup of coffee
first,—it will steady my nerves! [*Hebe has served the coffee, which
he drinks.*] So! [*Tears open the envelope and unfolds the letter.*]
Now for it!

Hebe. [*Placing her hand on his arm to restrain him from
reading the letter.*] Uncle, it may excite you too much!

Growler. It excites me a good deal more not to know what is

the matter with me!—To be or not to be,—that is the question!
[*Reads.*] "Dear sir and colleague!—This will be handed to you
by an incurable patient!" [*Frightened.*] What?

Hebe.   Oh, uncle,—that's preposterous!—You are not so sick as
all that!

Growler.   [*Dejectedly and feebly.*] I've always suspected it!—
I've felt it!—Incurable!—My head whirls,—I can read no further!
[*Drops the letter on the ground.*]

Hebe.   [*Picks up the letter.*] How could that man write such
nonsense? [*Reads.*] Why, uncle, you should have read farther,
—this isn't so bad as you think!

Growler.   Not so bad?—How could it possibly be worse?

Hebe.   Listen to this!—[*Reads as if continuing,*]—"incurable
patient."

Growler.   But why am I incurable?

Hebe.   [*Reading.*]   "He belongs to the category"—

Growler.   Now it's coming!

Hebe.   [*Reading.*]   "Of indefatigable self-observers, and
through the study of medical works has developed into an
imaginary chronic sufferer. In reality he is in perfect health."

Growler.   What's that?

Hebe.   [*Repeating*] "In reality he is in perfect health." Read
it yourself, uncle! [*Holding out the letter towards him.*]

Growler.   [*Pushing it away;—angrily.*] And that is what
that numskull dares to write?—I—in perfect health?

Hebe.   Why, uncle,—you ought to be glad to hear this!

Growler.   Then you believe what that fool writes?

Hebe.   [*Continuing to read.*] "If he insists on being ill, pre-
scribe harmless remedies, as I have done, and—as he is wealthy—
keep him under your care as long as possible!—Fraternally and
very sincerely yours, A. Kellum, M. D.!"

Growler.   [*Furiously.*] This is simply monstrous,—unheard
of! [*Rises.*] To say that I am in perfect health!—I think I ought
to know better myself!—Kellum should be sent to an insane
asylum!

Hebe.   But suppose he should be right, uncle!

Growler.   Are you going crazy too? Do you imagine I don't
know how I'm feeling myself? [*Taking the letter and tearing it
up.*] Bah,—the dolt,—the ignoramus,—the quack!—He's been
obtaining money under false pretenses!—The blood is rushing to
my head!—I can hear my heart beat! All my nerves are quiver-
ing!—Go, Hebe,—go quickly,—and get me a dose of bromo-
seltzer!

Hebe.   Yes, uncle,—at once! [*About to exit L.*]

Growler.   [*Calling her back.*] Hold on!—Wait a second!—
Bromo-seltzer alone won't be sufficient!—Get that medicine chest
out of my trunk!—I'll mix a nerve tonic myself!

Hebe.   All right, uncle! [*Exit quickly in hotel L.*]

Growler.   [*Calling after her.*] And order some chopped ice!—

What a lucky thing I read that letter!—The doctor here would never have believed that I am ill, if he had seen it!—I'm getting so hot,—I wonder if I am dressed too warmly!—[*Takes off his muffler.*] I had better take a little rest here before going inside! [*Sits down* R.]

Otto. [*Entering from hotel* L.] You vish to-day's morning paper, sir? All the latest news!

Growler. [*Grumbling.*] Do you think I want to read last week's papers with the stale news? Give it here! [*Takes paper from* Otto.]

Otto. Can I take the br-reakfast dings away?

Growler. You can, if you're strong enough to carry them!—[*Suddenly.*] See here, waiter, do I look like a man who is very ill?

Otto. [*Looking at him critically with the tray in his hands.*] You don't look at all well, sir!—But you'll get over it, if you stay here long enough! [Growler *holds out a dollar towards* Otto, *who places tray on table and pockets the money.*] Very much obliged to you, sir!—If dere's anything you vant, just call Otto, sir!—That's me! [*Picks up tray and goes towards* L. [*Aside.*] He likes to be told that he don't look well!—Next time he asks me how he looks, I'll tell him he's dying, und dat vill teeckle him to death, I bet you some! [*Exit in hotel* L.]

Growler. [*Opening the paper, looking after* Otto.] Notwithstanding his Teutonic brogue, that fellow seems to have some intelligence!—Hm!—Probably been an officer in the German army. [*Commences to read the paper.*]

Jones. [*Enters from hotel* L. *Remains on steps.*] He is alone! —Now is my chance! [*Coming down to* Growler.] Do you mind my taking this seat, sir?

Growler. [*Grumbling; turning his back towards him.*] It's none of my business!

Jones. [*Aside.*] Rather discouraging beginning,—but I won't give in so easily! [*After a short pause.*] Do you object to my lighting a cigarette, sir?

Growler. [*As before.*] There's no law here against the smoke nuisance.

Jones. [*Lighting a cigarette.*] I only smoke very mild Turkish cigarettes,—imported ones!—I detest the cheap domestic article!— Would you like to try one of these, sir? [*Offers him his cigarette case, and blows a mouthful of smoke towards him.*]

Growler. No, sir!—I want to preserve what little intellect nature has favored me with! [*Coughs.*] Hm!—hm! [*Rises.*] There's a draught here! [*Goes to* L. *and sits down at another table.*]

Jones. [*Rises also.*] Yes,—I believe you are right, sir!—I also thought I felt it.—One should always be careful of one's health! [*Sits down again near* Growler.]

Growler. [*Aside.*] He sticks like a porous plaster!

Jones. Are you affected with rheumatism, sir,—if I may ask?

Growler. If that were all!

Jones. According to the latest medical researches, it is claimed that rheumatism has its origin in an unhealthy condition of the liver, and from your appearance I should judge that your liver is not in its normal condition.—That's why I asked you! [*Short pause.*] They say Hot Springs is very good for rheumatic symptoms!

Growler. [*Surly, continuing to read the paper.*] I've been there!

Jones. Even better than West Baden!

Growler. I've been there!

Jones. Others prefer Saratoga!

Growler. I've been there!

Jones. Or the hot springs of Pasadena in California!

Growler. I've been there!

Jones. It is very interesting to hear that you have visited all these resorts, but still more interesting to become personally acquainted with you, sir!—We shall probably be thrown a great deal in each other's company during our stay here, and I should like very much to profit by your experience!—Will you allow me to introduce myself?

Growler. [*Waving him off.*] No, sir!

Jones. My name is —

Growler. [*Interrupting him.*] No, sir!—No, sir!—I don't care what your name is!—I don't wish to make your acquaintance, nor any one else's!—I have enough to do to attend to my own troubles! [*Turns his back towards him.*]

Jones. In that case, I beg your pardon!—I hope you will excuse my intrusion!

Growler. Don't mention it!

Jones. [*Rises and moves to* R. *Aside.*] Unapproachable as a bear, and hermetically sealed like a torpedo. [*Stands* R, *watching* Growler, *who first seems absorbed in the reading of his newspaper, then gradually turns towards* R., *slowly lowers the paper and peeps over the edge of it towards* Jones. *Their eyes meet, and* Growler *quickly raises the paper again.*] Excuse me,—I'll no longer intrude upon you, sir! [*Goes up stage.*—**Dr. Rogers** *enters* R. U. E. *and simultaneously* **Otto** *from hotel* L. *They meet in* C. *of stage.*]

Otto. Och, doctor,—here you vos at last!—There is dot old gendleman, Mr. Gr-rowler, who vonted to see' you so badly! [*Points towards* Growler *down stage* L.]

Dr. Rogers. All right Otto! [*Approaches* Growler *who has turned his back again towards* R. *and is reading his paper.*] Good morning, sir!—Let me introduce myself!—I am————

Growler. [*Jumping up, angrily.*] Ten thousand devils!—This is getting too much!—Can't a man find a moment's rest here?—I don't wish to make anybody's acquaintance in this place!—Is that plain enough, sir?

Dr. Rogers. [*Smiling.*] Perfectly, sir,—but I am——

Growler. I don't care a continental who you are, sir!—It seems that the only occupation the people here have, is to introduce hemselves!

Otto. But oxcuse me, Mr. Gr-rowler, dis is Dr. Rogers, whom you vonted to see so badly already dis morning so early!

Growler. Then why didn't you say so at once, you idiot? [*Very politely to* **Dr. Rogers.**] I hope you will pardon my abrupt-ness, my dear doctor! [*They shake hands.*] I have been annoyed just now by a very obtrusive young man, who persisted ——— [*Sees* **Jones** *up stage.*] Oh, there he is still!

Jones. Go ahead, sir,—don't mind me!—My feelings are iron-clad and bullet proof. [*Exit slowly* L. U. E.]

Growler. [*Not deigning to notice* **Jones** *any further.*] So you see, doctor,—my nerves are somewhat upset!—Besides I have had other things to vex me this morning!—When a man is almost continually suffering from one ailment or another, like myself, he should be pardoned for not always being in a pleasant and con-genial humor!

Dr. Rogers. Certainly,—certainly, my dear sir!—As a medical man I can fully sympathise with you?—But kindly explain to me what seem to be your principal symptoms!

Growler. That's not a very easy thing to do, doctor! My entire system seems to be undermined! My appetite is very poor and my digestion worse!—Before taking the train in Chicago yesterday I had for dinner only a plate of turtle soup, some fried fish, a hamburger steak with onions, an omelet with ham, a veal cutlet with potato salad, some Roquefort cheese, a couple of pieces of apple pie, and three, or maybe four cups of coffee, and a plate of ice cream!—Would you believe it that on the train, and after my arrival here, I had a most alarming feeling of oppression, as if there was a heavy weight upon me?

Dr. Rogers. Yes, I can understand that!

Growler. And then my liver doesn't seem to be in proper order,—and my heart goes either too slow or too fast!

Dr. Rogers. Any other symptoms?

Growler. Don't you think, doctor, those are about enough?

Dr. Rogers. Well, I have no doubt that with proper care, a punctual attention to our orders and prescriptions, and the systematic use of Silurian water, we will make a new man out of you, Mr. Growler!

Growler. I hope so, doctor!—But first of all, I would like you to make a careful and thorough examination of my entire system!

Dr. Rogers. Very well, sir!—We will do so now, if you like! [*Points towards the hotel*] Let us go to your room!

Growler. Yes, let us go at once! [*They go towards hotel* L.] I want you also to use your stethoscope, doctor!

Dr. Rogers. Of course, sir,—of course! [*Exeunt* **Growler** *and* **Dr. Rogers** *in hotel* L. *During the previous scene* **Mildred** *and* **Vivian**, *with an open letter in her hand, have entered from hotel* L., *and have been ushered by* Otto *to seats in the arbor* L. **Vivian** *is reading the letter.* Otto *exit in hotel* L.]

Mildred. Why, Vivian,—that's the third time you are reading that letter!

Vivian. I think it was so nice of Fred to write me the same day we left!

Mildred. That's no reason you should try to commit his letter to memory!

Vivian. There would be no harm in it if I did, aunt!

Mildred. Yes, there would be!

Vivian. Poor, boy,—this is the second day he has had to eat his breakfast all alone! [*Pensively.*] I wonder how he is getting along!

Mildred. He is probably commencing to long for you,—and it will be a good thing for him, if he does!

Vivian. But I am longing for him just as much!

Mildred. I took you along with me to have a cheerful companion,—not to hear your lamentations about your Fred from morning till night!—For heaven's sake, Vivian,—do let up on him for a little while!—If you were with him now, you would probably be quarreling again!—I am going to take you for a drive to Pewaukee Lake after breakfast!—That may put you in a better humor! [*Short pause.*] Did you hear what I was saying, Vivian?

Vivian. [*Absent mindedly.*] Yes, auntie,—I did!

Mildred. Perhaps Mr. Jones would like to accompany us. He seems to be a perfect gentleman!—How polite, obliging and courteous he was on the train!

Vivian. [*As before.*] Yes auntie!

[*Enter* **Fred**, *clean shaven, with a curly blonde wig, in a light summer suit, carrying a large satchel and an ulster,* R. U. E.—Jones *re-enters* L. U. E.]

Fred. Here we are! [*Calling.*] I say, waiter!

Vivian. [*Nervously grabbing* **Mildred's** *arm.*] Oh,—aunt Mildred!

Mildred. [*Startled.*] What's the matter with you, Vivian?

Vivian. That sounded like Fred's voice!

Mildred. [*Coolly.*] You seem to have Fred on the brain!

Otto. [*Who has entered from hotel, and has been conversing with* Fred, *and taken the satchel and coat.*] Yes, sir!—This way to the office, sir! [*Exeunt* Fred *and* Otto *in hotel* L.]

Vivian. No, aunt,—I am sure, it was exactly like his voice! [*Rises and steps from arbor to* R., *to see who the speaker is, and meets* Jones, *who has come down stage.*]

Jones. [*Bowing and taking off his hat.*] Ah, good morning, Mrs. Parker!

Vivian. Good morning, Mr. Jones!—Did you see the gentleman who just entered the hotel?

Jones. Yes, madam,—I did.

Vivian. Did you know him?

Jones. No!

Vivian. Then it wasn't my husband!

Jones. [*Astonished.*] Your husband? [*Both have gone to* L. *and have arrived near the arbor.*]

Mildred. My niece is having day dreams, Mr. Jones.

Vivian. [*To* Jones.] Didn't his voice sound like my husband's to you, Mr. Jones?

Jones. If you wish it, I'll go to the office and find out from the clerk who the gentleman is!

Mildred. If you will be so kind sir!—My niece's mind won't be at rest till she's found out the absurdity of her imagination! [Jones, *exit in hotel* L.] You are so entirely wrapped up in your husband, Vivian, that I'm afraid yours is a hopeless case!—He'll boss you, as long as you live!—I'd like to see the man who could play the tyrant over me, if I were married!

Vivian. If you were married, auntie,—you might love your husband just as much as I do mine!

Mildred. I might,—or I might not!—That would depend on circumstances!—But if I did, I would certainly not make a holy show of myself on account of it, like you do!—The idea of Fred being here!—Now what could possibly make him leave his business in Chicago, and come here on a fool's errand?

Vivian. Simply his love for me, auntie!

Mildred. Say rather his jealousy, and his fear of your flirting with some one else!

Vivian. Oh, aunt Mildred,—how absurd!—How could he possibly get such a foolish idea into his head?

Mildred. Oh, I don't know!—There's nothing absurd about it! —Only the other day when we were alone, he remarked that you were rather prettier than he cared to have you, as it attracted the attention of so many other men!

Vivian. He said that?—Then he mistrusts me!—I think that's an insult to me!

Jones. [*Entering from hotel* L.] That gentleman's name is Harrison,—Mrs. Parker!—Gerald Harrison, artist, from Milwaukee!

Mildred. [*To* Vivian.] I hope you're satisfied now!

Vivian. [*Somewhat disappointed.*] Thank you, Mr. Jones!

Jones. [*Looking towards hotel.*] Ah, here he comes now!— Excuse me, ladies,—I have a letter to write which I want to send by the next train!—If there is anything I can do for you, please send to my room, and I will be at your service! [*The ladies nod to him, he bows to them and goes up stage to* L. *towards hotel. On the steps he meets* Fred, *who enters from hotel. In passing him.*] Good morning, sir! [*Exit in hotel* L.]

Fred. [*Coming down the steps.*] Good morning! [*Aside.*] He didn't recognize me!—Good! [*Goes to arbor* l. *and sees the ladies inside.*] Oh,—excuse me, ladies! [*Aside.*] Now to be on my guard! [*Goes to* r. *sits down at a table, and takes out a newspaper.*]

Vivian. [*Softly to* **Mildred.**] Aunt,—it is Fred,—I'm sure!—It's his walk exactly!

Mildred. Nonsense!—Fred has a full beard!

Vivian. He has shaved it off!—Only—I have never seen him wear a suit like that!

Mildred. That he could easily have bought!—But it's an easy matter to find out whether it is Fred or not! [*Rises.*] Just watch him! [*Goes to* c. *and turns up stage, calling:*] Fred!

Fred. [*Holding the newspaper in front of him;—aside.*] Yes, go ahead!—Holler your lungs out, you old catamaran!

Mildred. [*Louder.*] Fred!—Fred!

Fred. [*Still louder.*] Oh, Fred! [*To* **Mildred.**] You want a waiter, madam?

Mildred. No, thank you sir!

Fred. Excuse me, madam! [*Stares at* **Mildred** *with wide open eyes.*]

Mildred. [*Returning to the arbor* l. *Aside.*] I really believe it is Fred!—The way he stared at me reminds me of the malicious glances he honors me with when at home! [*To* **Vivian.**] Vivy, —you were right! It is he! [*Sits down again.*] Oh, just you wait, Mr. Fred!

Growler. [*Entering from hotel* l. *accompanied by* **Hebe.**] Now, Hebe,—try and remember all the doctor's orders!—At eight in the morning—three glasses of spring water,—then one hour's walk!

Hebe. Then your breakfast,—very light!

Growler. Hm!—Did he say so?

Hebe. Oh, yes,—uncle!—I'm sure!

Growler. Well, at eleven more water, and a hot bath, followed by a cold shower!

Hebe. Then you'll have to lie down for an hour before your lunch,—also light!

Growler. Hm,—yes!—I suppose so!—Then after lunch he'll give me electric treatment!—Before retiring—a sponge bath!—Now—there's a doctor who understands his profession!—He keeps me busy pretty near all day, but I may expect some results from his treatment!

Hebe. [*Motioning towards arbor* l.] Uncle,—there is Miss Green and her niece! Won't you speak to them and thank them for their kindness?

Growler. No,—no!—That medical examination has worn me out!—You can do so later on!—I am in need of some rest now! [*Sits down* r. *at a table behind* **Fred.**] Come, sit down here! [**Hebe** *sits down beside him. Enter* **Jones** *from hotel* l.] Don't turn round just now, Hebe,—but there's that officious individual, of whom I had such trouble to get rid a little while ago!

Hebe. [*Slowly turning round and looking over her shoulder towards* Jones *who is approaching the arbor* L.] Ah. is that he?

Jones. [*To* Mildred *and* Vivian.] So,—my correspondence is finished!—Will the ladies permit me to keep them company? [*The ladies smile and nod.* Jones *takes a seat beside* Vivian.]

Fred. [*Watching them behind his newspaper:—aside.*] They seem on a rather familiar footing! [*Grunting.*] Hm!--it didn't take them long!

Mildred. [*Rising.*] I hope you'll excuse me for a little while, Mr. Jones,—but I have an appointment with Dr. Rogers!—After I get through with him, we'll take our drive, Vivian! [*Smiles and nods to* Jones, *throws an inquisitive glance towards* Fred, *and exit in hotel* L.]

Fred. [*Aside.*] The old fool—to leave those two alone!

Jones. My dear Mrs. Parker,—I am glad to find an opportunity to see you alone for a moment!—I have something on my mind, and would like to explain to you why I have followed you here.

Vivian. You followed me?—I thought you came here for your health!

Jones. To be candid with you—there is no health resort in existence, which could cure my malady!

Vivian. [*Astonished.*] Ah!

Jones. Since I called at your house, day before yesterday,—I am suffering here! [*Points at his heart.*]

Fred. [*Who has caught his words;—aside.*] I'll kill that impudent scoundrel!

Jones. [*Softly to* Vivian.) I am in love,—head over heels in love—[*Pointing stealthily towards* Hebe,] with that little lady over there!—Will you assist me in furthering my suit?

Fred. [*Eagerly listening;—aside.*] I can't hear a word anymore of what he's saying, confound it!

Vivian. [*Watching* Fred;—*aside.*] How he is watching us!— Ah,—I've found a way to get absolute assurance of his identity!

Jones. May I count on your assistance, Mrs. Parker?

Vivian. Yes,—I'll aid you to the best of my ability.—on one condition!

Jones. State anything in my power!

Vivian. [*Bending towards* Jones,--*softly.*] I want you to find out if that gentleman's name is really Harrison!

Fred. [*Watching them.*] They're getting still more familiar! —I can't stand this much longer!

Jones. Shall I go and ask him?

Vivian. Oh, no!—All I want is to have a look at the initials on that handkerchief in his breast pocket!

Jones. Then you want me to———[*Makes a gesture indicating a pickpocket.*]

Vivian. That's it exactly!

Jones. It's a little risky,—but I'll do it for her sake! [*Looks towards* **Fred.**]

Fred. [*Aside.*] It seems they would like to have me out of the way!

Jones. Well,—nothing risked—nothing gained!—Luckily I am pretty good at sleight-of-hand tricks! [*Rises and approaches* **Fred,** *who hides himself behind his newspaper, and turns his back towards him.*] Sir,—my name is Jones!

Fred. [*Surly.*] Mine is Harrison!

Jones. I see you are reading the Record;—would you mind letting me have a look at it, after you get through with it?

Fred. Not at all, sir! [*Beckons* **Jones** *to bend over him;—softly.*] The face of that lady at your table seems familiar to me!—Would you be kind enough to tell me her name?

Jones. [*While bending over* **Fred** *is gradually pulling his handkerchief out of his breast-pocket, unperceived by the latter.*] Certainly, sir!—The lady's name is Mrs. Parker, the wife of a wholesale dry goods merchant of Chicago.—Rather an attractive appearance, hasn't she?

Fred. [*Sarcastically.*] Yes,—rather!—Would you mind giving me an introduction to her later on?

Jones. With the greatest pleasure, sir! [*He pulls out* **Fred's** *handkerchief and hides it behind his back, but is caught in the action by* **Hebe,** *who has been watching him.*]

Hebe. [*Startled.*] Heaven,—what's that I see!

Growler. What's the matter? [*Both rise.*] Am I looking worse, you think?

Hebe. No, no, uncle,—nothing of the kind! [*Sadly, aside.*] A common pickpocket!—Who would have thought that? [*Exit quickly* R.]

Growler. [*Excitedly.*] What's that she's mumbling? I wonder what's the matter?—Can I be looking worse,—and she's trying to hide it from me?—Is that why she's running away from me so fast? I must find out! [*Exit quickly after* **Hebe** R.]

Jones. [*Returning to* **Vivian** L., *and giving her the stolen handkerchief.*] Here is the mute proof of my dishonor,—the silent witness of the first blotch on my hitherto stainless escutcheon!

Vivian. [*Looking at the initials in one of the corners of the handkerchief. Aside.*] ' F. P.''—It is Fred!

Jones. Well, Mrs. Parker? Did you find out what you wanted to know?

Vivian. [*Dissembling.*] No,—it was a disappointment!—The initials are not what I expected them to be!

Jones. Then hadn't I better return the *corpus delicti?*

Vivian. No,—I won't trouble you again! Bye and bye, when he isn't looking, I'll throw it under his chair!

Jones. He asked me who you were just now!

Vivian. Indeed?

Jones. And he wanted to be introduced to you!

Vivian. [*Aside.*] What impudence!

Jones. Do you object?

Vivian. Oh,—not at all! [*Jones goes to Fred and converses with him.*] So,—he suspects me of being a flirt, and wants to to play the spy on me! He deserves to be punished!—Here he comes now! [*Jones and Fred approach Vivian.*]

Jones. [*Introducing.*] Mrs. Parker,—allow me to introduce Mr. Harrison to you!

Vivian. [*Observing him critically.*] Mr. Harrison?

Fred. [*Quickly.*] Artist,—from Milwaukee, Madam!

Vivian. Ah!—Artist?

Fred. I sincerely hope I am not intruding?

Jones. Now, Mrs. Parker, will you kindly pardon me if I retire to attend to a little business matter? [*Bows and goes up stage.*] I'll try one more attack on old Growler! [*Looks round as if in search of Growler, and exit R.*]

Fred. You must think me rather bold to have asked for the favor of an introduction to you, Mrs. Parker,—but you will admit that etiquette is not so strictly observed in these places;—therefore I hope you'll pardon the liberty I took!—Besides, my occupation as painter, gives me the privilege to go in quest of everything that is beautiful in nature!

Vivian. If your portraits are as flattering as your conversation. Mr. Harrison, your talents must be in great demand.

Fred. Pardon me,—I merely stated a fact, and did not attempt to flatter.—If not too inquisitive, may I ask if Mr. Parker is also here?

Vivian. No, sir!—My husband's business detains him in Chicago!

Fred. It must surely have been a great sacrifice on his part to let you travel without him!

Vivian. On the contrary, sir.—he let me go *with the greatest pleasure!* As for myself, I am only too happy to escape for once the monotony of our home, and to enjoy some liberty!

Fred. Ah!—Then I surmise that your husband is inclined to play the tyrant!

Vivian. Not quite so bad as that!—But he has other faults—nearly as bad,—for he is arbitrary, quarrelsome, and irritable!

Fred. In that case I sympathize with you most sincerely!

Vivian. I believe I deserve some sympathy,—for hardly a day passes by but we have a few———well,———that we are of a different opinion on some subject or another, and have a scene.

Fred. Excuse me,—but is your husband alone to blame?

Vivian. Most decidedly!—Before our marriage I had the sweetest temper imaginable, and got along amicably with everybody!—Even now I am on the best of terms with my aunt, and —Mr. Jones! —

Fred. [*Ironically,*] Yes, madam,—you seem to be on most excellent terms with Mr. Jones!

Vivian. [*Mischievously.*] He is such a nice, agreeable young man!—A perfect gentleman,—always obliging, polite, attentive, entertaining and full of fun!

Fred. [*Hardly able to restrain his anger.*] Ah,—indeed?—I shall be glad to get better acquainted with Mr. Jones!

Vivian. He is so even tempered,—never irritable!—And after what I told you of my husband, Mr. Harrison,—you can easily imagine how I must appreciate that quality in a man!—Are you a married man?

Fred. Thank heaven—no, madam!

Vivian. Thank heaven—no? That is scarcely polite in my presence, sir!

Fred. I beg your pardon!—I didn't mean it that way!—In you I might have found the ideal I have till now searched for in vain!

Vivian. Really?—What a pity we did not meet before!—And what special qualifications is your ideal to be possessed of, if I may ask?

Fred. First of all—she must be as beautiful as an angel,—as artist I am surely entitled to that!—Furthermore she must be of a home-loving disposition, sweet tempered and of a soft and yielding nature, willing always to bow to a man's superior intelligence!

Vivian. Even when that man is wrong?

Fred. Even then!—Especially then!—That's exactly where her yielding nature would have to come in!—Then she would have to refrain from receiving the attention of any other man, nor think them agreeable and entertaining!

Vivian. Indeed? Then let me offer you one piece of advice,—since you are an artist, if I were in your place,—I would paint such a paragon of modesty and virtue, and marry her. [*Rises excitedly.*]

Fred. [*Also rising.*] I hope our conversation has not annoyed you!

Vivian. I must admit that it has!—It has brought back to me too many unpleasant recollections of my home troubles!

Fred. I am truly sorry if I have grieved you!

Vivian. It is a deplorable fact that men expect everything from us, and are unwilling in their turn to make any concessions whatever!—I am afraid we would not harmonize very well together, Mr. Harrison!—I must admit that Mr. Jones' good qualities are more acceptable to me! [*Exit quickly in hotel* L.]

Fred. And that's what I've got to swallow!—My own wife to tell me that she prefers another man to me!—But wait till the moment of dissimulation is past!—Like an avenging angel I'll step between them, and wither them with the thunder of my wrath!

Jones. [*Enters* R. U. E., *goes to arbor* L. *and looks into it.*] Ah, —Mrs. Parker gone?

Fred. Yes,—she went inside!

Jones. Charming woman, isn't she?

Fred. [*Nervously handling his cane and suppressing his anger.*] Yes,—very!

Jones. We came here on the same train, and from the very start I took a great fancy to her!

Fred. Are you acquainted with her husband?

Jones. Only slightly!—Seems to be an erratic, irritable sort of a chap!

Fred. I can easily guess the rest! You are surely not here for your health! At least you don't look like it!

Jones. [*Laughing.*] No,—there's nothing the matter with me! I'm as strong as a mule! [*Pointing at his heart.*] My only trouble is here!—And I believe I'll find a remedy for that while here!

Fred. [*Swinging his cane.*] I hope you won't address yourself to the wrong doctor!

Jones. What are you swinging your cane for so continually?

Fred. Only a habit of mine!—To keep my wrist supple!

Jones. Do you need that as an artist?

Fred. Yes,—to paint faces!

Jones. Ah,—you are a portrait painter?—Then you are just my man!—I would like very much to have a miniature of my lady love; but strictly on the q. t., of course!

Fred. Ah!

Jones. I'll sit down beside her, so she'll have a pleasant expression, and you can make a sketch of her unobserved by anyone!

Fred. [*Aside.*] I cannot contain myself much longer! [*Aloud.*] This may cost you dear, sir!

Jones. Oh, I don't mind that!—It's immaterial!—As long as it is a good likeness!

Jones. [*Sternly.*] It will be the best job I have ever done in my life,—I promise you that!—Good morning, Mr. Jones! [*Exit in hotel* L., *making passes with his cane.*]

Jones. I'll see you later, Mr. Harrison! [*Rubbing his hands.*] Splendid!

Hebe. [*Entering quickly* R. U. E.] There he is now, sir!

Jones. [*Agreeably surprised.*] Hebe!—Miss Worthy!

Hebe. I have run ahead of my uncle to speak to you!

Jones. How kind of you! [*About to take her hand.*]

Hebe. [*Shrinking away from him.*] Do not touch me, please! —I have nothing but contempt for you!

Jones. [*Astonished*] Contempt for me?

Hebe. Let me advise you to leave here as soon as possible!

Jones. Leave—while you are here?

Hebe. No more of this, sir!—I shall not betray you, but you must go at once! [*Goes up stage to meet her uncle, who enters* R. U. E.]

Jones. What the deuce does she mean?—I leave here at once? —Why?—She has nothing but contempt for me?—What can that old, walking medicine chest have told her about me?—There he sits down!—Now is my time!—I'll make my last attempt to get acquainted with him!

Hebe. I'll get your shawl, uncle! [*Exit in hotel* L.]

Jones. [*Going towards hotel, calling.*] I say,—waiter! [*Very loud.*] Oh, waiter!

Growler. [*Covering his ears with his hands.*] Why the dickens does that fellow howl so?

Otto. [*Entering quickly from hotel* L.] Did you call sir?—Did you vont me?

Jones. Do you think I called you because I didn't want you?

Otto. Sometimes dey do so already, sir!

Jones. Get me a masseur!

Otto. What kind of dings, sir?

Jones. A masseur, stupid!—A person who understands massage treatment!

Otto. I never heard of dose things, sir!

Jones. Never heard of massage treatment in a health resort? [**Growler** *becomes interested.*]

Otto. No, sir,—I bet you some!

Jones. Impossible!—Not heard of the latest scientific method of curing disease by systematic manipulations? The only successful treatment in cases of paralysis, neuralgia, rheumatism and joint diseases? And you call this an up to date sanitorium? It's incredible,—preposterous! [*Aside.*] If the old shark don't tackle the bait now, I'll throw up the sponge! [*To* **Otto.**] Very well,—I'll have to go where they are up to the times!—It seems you are fifty years behind here! [**Otto** *exit in hotel* L. *shaking his head, and shrugging his shoulders.*]

Growler. [*Has become more and more interested, rises, and approaches* **Jones.**] Excuse me, sir,—I heard you speak of the only successful treatment of neuralgia and rheumatism! This interests me!

Jones. [*Stiffly.*] Pardon me, sir!—I have not the pleasure of your acquaintance!

Growler. [*Humbly.*] My name is Growler, sir!—Jeremiah Growler, from Chicago!

Jones. [*Quickly.*] My name is James Jones,—lately from Joplin, Missouri;—it is my intention to establish myself in Chicago in the drug business;—I am twenty-six years old,—am a member of the Episcopal Church,—not without means,—with considerable expectations in the future from a wealthy uncle, who is single——

Growler. [*Interrupting him.*] Very glad to hear it,—but I meant to ask you in regards to that infallible cure you mentioned just now!

Jones. Oh,—the massage treatment, you mean? [*Makes the motions of a masseur.*]

Growler. Yes,—that's it! [*Imitates* **Jones'** *movements.*] I never heard of it before!

Jones. You astonish me!—It's universally known and used now-a-days! It's almost magical in its effects!—The cuticle the nerve and muscular system are thoroughly kneaded, according to scientific methods,—the blood flows freely through the arteries, and brings health and vigor to all afflicted organs.

Growler. Health and vigor?—My dear sir, you bring me hope at last! You can scarcely imagine how I have suffered!—For years my life has been one of agony and pain!—My entire system is undermined!

Jones. In that case massage treatment will be your only salvation!—I have used it, and see how healthy I am!—Even after the first treatment you will feel as light as a bird in the air, ready to fly!

Growler. [*Sighing.*] And just to think that nobody here understands it!—How unfortunate!

Jones. Ah,—but luckily I do,—and I dare to say thoroughly! I have made a study of it, and if you will only permit me——

Growler. [*Gladly.*] My dear sir,—I would consider it a great favor!

Jones. I am entirely at your service!—And if it benefits you, I will give you a treatment every day!—Please, be seated here! [*Places a chair in c. of stage, and another one in front of it.*]

Growler. What?—Here in the open air?

Jones. Only by way of experiment! [**Growler** *sits down* c.] Now, place your feet on the other chair, and bend your body backwards!—So!—In case you have rheumatism in the shoulder-blades and arms,—this is the treatment! [*Kneads his shoulders and arms.*] So! [*Continues the massage.*]

Growler. [*Grunting.*] Oh!—Ah!—I feel relieved already!—It is wonderful!—Oh!—Oh!

Jones. [*While kneading.*] Mr. Growler,—I saw you in the company of a young lady this morning!—May I ask——?

Growler. Never mind the young lady!—Let us stick to the treatment!—Oh!

Jones. Very well!—Now, lean back a little further, and I will operate on the muscles of the chest! [*Kneads his chest.*]

Growler. [*Squirming.*] Oh!—Ah!—Ahaha!—Your are tickling me!

Jones. Only a slight irritation which you must overcome!—You will get used to it!

Growler. Yes,—yes, I see!—Oh!—Ah!

Jones. It does you good, eh? [*Continuing to knead.*]

Growler. Yes,—oh, yes!—Oh!—Ah!—Please,—stop!—Ahaha!—I can——not——stand——anymore!

Jones. Only a little more willpower!—It's nothing when you're used to it!

Growler. Oh!—Ah!—Ahaha! [*Becomes hysterical.*]

Hebe. [*Enters from hotel* L. *with a shawl on her arm.* **She** *sees her uncle and* **Jones** *and starts in fright.*] Good heavens,—he is killing my uncle!—Help! –Murder!—Help! [*Enter all the characters from hotel and* R. U. E, *while* **Jones** *continues to operate on* **Growler.** **Hebe** *faints in* **Fred's** *arms.*]

Picture—Quick Curtain.

ACT III.

SCENE : **Fred Parker's** *room in the Park Hotel at Waukesha —The usual hotel bedroom furniture.—Door* C.—*Window* R.—*A door supposed to lead to* **Growler's** *room* L.—*This door must open inward and up stage.—As the curtain rises, enter* **Harrison,** *a very stout man with a florid complexion,* C. D.—*He comes down stage, leaving the door open, and looks around.*

Harrison. So,—these will be quarters for the next two weeks to come!—Not overluxurious, but I'll have to put up with it!—So long as I can get rid of twenty or thirty pounds avoirdupois while here, I'll be satisfied! [*Sits down.*]

Otto. [*Entering* C. D.] Oxcuse me, sir,—but there was a mistake made by the bell boy.—He vos a new boy und showed you de wrong room.—Your room is anodder room.—I will show you already!—It's next door on de odder side!

Harrison. Well,—then I suppose I'll have to move again! [*Grunts.*] Here,—give me a lift! [**Otto** *assists him to rise.* **Harrison** *exit* C. D. **Otto** *is about to follow him when* **Fred** *enters.*]

Fred. What is that man doing in my room?

Otto. Only a mistake, Mr. Harrison!—Dot gentleman joost come, und got in de wrong room!—He is going to his own room already, I told him!—Dere vos a telegraph in de office for you, sir!

Fred. A telegram?—Bring it up at once!

Otto. Yes, sir! [*Exit* C. D. *closing it.*]

Fred. That must be from Torrence!—He is the only person who knows that I am here! [*Goes to window* R.] There's Vivian now sitting in the garden,—and all alone!—I wonder where that lovely aunt of hers is!—Oh, but she's a good guardian to have over one's wife!—Just wait till Mr. Jones gets fresh again, and I'll soon settle his hash!

Otto. [*Enters* C. D., *after knocking, with a telegram.*] Here vos de telegraph already, sir!

Fred. [*Taking it.*] Wait a moment!—There may be an answer!
[*Opens telegram and reads.*] "Your personal property tax fixed
at $7,000. Are you satisfied?—Will." [*Astonished.*] What?—My
personal property tax $7,000 a year? Have I suddenly become a
millionaire? [*Sits down at table* c., *on which are writing
materials.*] Ah, here's a Western Union blank! [*Writes, while
repeating the words aloud.*] "Wm. Torrence—Parker & Torrence
—Chicago—Illinois—Have you gone crazy or are you making a
fool of me.—Fred." [*Counts the words from one to ten, and rises.*]
There!—Tell them to rush it!—Collect!

Otto. Yes, sir!—All right, sir! [*Exit* c. d. *Enter immediately
after his exit,* Growler & Hebe *from* c. d.]

Growler. [*Coming down stage.*] Excuse our intrusion, sir!

Fred. What can I do for you, sir?

Growler. I occupied this room last night, but they gave me
another one this morning. I fear I lost something in here!

Hebe. My uncle's pocketbook is missing, sir!

Fred. Sorry, but I haven't seen it. Please look for yourself!
[*Goes to window* r. *and looks out.*]

Growler. Search everywhere, Hebe!—Your eyes are better
than mine!

Hebe. [*Searching.*] I can find it nowhere!

Growler. Hand me that cane over there! [*Hebe hands him
Fred's cane. He stoops and searches with it under the sofa* L.
Suddenly crying out.] Ah!

Hebe. Did you find it uncle?

Growler. [*Sinks down on the sofa rubbing his side.* Fred.
turns round to him.] A stitch in my side! Pardon me, sir,—I'll
soon get over it, I hope!

Fred. [*Nodding his head.*] So do I! Don't hurry on my
account! [*Turns back to the window.*]

Growler. [*To Hebe who continues to search.*] Can't you find
it anywhere, Hebe?

Hebe. You may take my word for it, uncle!—I'm sure that
young man took it from you!

Growler. [*Rising with difficulty, and as if in pain.*] Bah!—
Nonsense!--He was only giving me a massage treatment!

Hebe. I did not intend to tell you this, but after all I think I
had better!

Growler. What are you driving at?

Hebe. That massage treatment was only a pretext.—I have
seen him do some other of his tricks.—Come, uncle, there's no
use to search here any longer,—we are only in this gentleman's
way.

Growler. [*Loudly.*] Just to think that we should have fallen
here among robbers!

Fred. [*Quickly turning round.*] Do you mean to accuse me,
sir?

Hebe. Oh, not at all, sir!--Please excuse my uncle's excitement!

Growler. You go ahead, Hebe! -I want to explain to this gentleman that it is not a question of lost money! [Hebe *exit* c. d.]

Fred. Not of lost money?—Then it can certainly not be of much consequence!

Growler. There is where you are mistaken, sir!—I am a constant invalid, and that pocketbook was full of useful receipts!

Fred. Then you may thank your lucky stars that you lost it!—It's too much doctoring that makes people ill!

Growler. If you knew my unfortunate condition, you wouldn't speak like that!—I am suffering from————

Fred. [*Interrupting him.*] We all have to bear our troubles, I suppose!

Growler. Ah, yes,—of course!—May I ask what your symptoms are? [*Takes a chair and sits down.*] Now, tell me all about yourself!--Afterwards I will give you an idea of what ails me!

Fred. [*Scarcely restraining himself.*] Pardon me, but I can not listen to you, sir,————I

Growler. Yes, I must admit it is painful to hear the recital of my many ailments!

Fred. You misunderstand me, sir!—I have neither time nor inclination to hear any more of your complaints!—My nerves are somewhat upset!

Growler. [*Rising.*] I regret to hear it!—That is also one of my greatest troubles!—Well, my list of misfortunes will have to keep till some other time!—We could take a nice, long walk together, when I will be better able to give you a complete diagnosis!

Fred. [*Driving him towards* c. d.] Yes, yes,—some other day! I have no time now!

Growler. It would probably not take me more than two hours to tell you all about it!

Fred. It will greatly interest me no doubt!—Only not now!

Growler. [*Near* c. d., *offering his hand.*] My dear sir, I am so glad to have met you!

Fred. [*Shaking his hand energetically.*] The pleasure is mutual!

Growler. [*As if in pain.*] Ah!—Oh!—Good day, sir!

Fred. [*Slamming the door.*] I thought I never would get rid of that bore!

Growler. [*Reopening the door.*] Pardon me,—I only wanted to inform you that I am your next door neighbor, No. 13! [*Pointing to door* l.] That door there leads to my room!

Fred. [*Angrily.*] All right! [**Growler** *shuts the door again.*] If he comes back again I'll murder him! [*Goes to window* r.] Still alone!—Where the dickens is her aunt? I'll have to see to this myself! [*Goes to* c. *and is met by* **Otto,** *who enters.*]

Otto. [*Somewhat confused.*] Ach. oxcuse me, Mr. Harrison,--I think you have gone out already! [*Is about to leave when called back by* **Fred.**]

Fred. Here,—come back!—What did you want in here?

Otto. [*Snickering.*] Dere's a lady oudside!

Fred. Well,—what does she want of me?

Otto. [*Same business.*] He-he-he!—I dink you make a mash on her,—I bet you some!

Fred. What rubbish are you talking?—What does she want? —Out with it!

Otto. He-he-he!—I've promised not to tell, sir!—He-he-he!

Fred. See here,—if you don't tell me, I'll break every bone in your body!

Otto. Ach, no, sir!—I vont like dat!—It's really too funny for anydings, I bet you!—She vants some piece of your linen for a souffenir!—He-he-he!

Fred. Is she crazy?

Otto. Yes, sir,—I dink so!—Und she is not very young neither already yet!

Fred. Who is the lady?

Otto. No. 34!—I mean Miss Green!

Fred. Ah!—I don't know her!

Otto. Will you let her have dat souffenir, sir?

Fred. Most decidedly not!—And if you dare to sneak anything out of this room, I'll have you discharged on the spot,—do you hear? [*Goes threateningly towards* Otto.]

Otto. [*Frightened.*] All right, sir!—I vont touch anydings in here, I bet you some. [*Exit* c. d.]

Fred. Aha!—Aunt Mildred is on my track!—It's well to be forewarned! [*Looking around.*] Luckily I left nothing lying loose around here! [*Goes to his satchel near window* r. *and tries the lock.*] And my satchel is safely locked!—Now, I'll go down to Vivian! [*Takes up his hat and cane.*]

Otto. [*Enters* c. d.] Ach, Mr. Harrison!

Fred. Now,—what is it you want again?

Otto. Dot lady says she vont to speak mit you.—Can she come in?

Fred. Not on your life!—I don't receive visits from ladies!

Otto. Not when dey're old already, I suppose!—Vot shall I tell her?

Fred. Anything you please!

Otto. I'll tell her you vos in your bathtup!—Then she von't come, I bet you some! [*Exit quickly* c. d.]

Fred. The trail is getting hot, and dear auntie is persistent!— But I'll lose no more time here, while Mr. Jones may be making himself agreeable to my wife! [*Picks up his hat and cane again and is about to leave when* Dr. Rogers *enters* c. d.]

Dr. Rogers. Pardon me,—have I the pleasure to see Mr. Harrison?

Fred. That's my name, sir!

Dr. Rogers. I am Dr. Rogers! [*Puts down his hat.*] Your valet informed me just now of your arrival!

Fred. My valet?

Dr. Rogers. I received your letter from Chicago yesterday, but expected you on a later train.

Fred. See here, doctor,—there must be a mistake!—I never wrote to you in my life!

Dr. Rogers. In that case there must be another guest by your name stopping here!

Fred. Very likely!—Harrison is not an uncommon name!

Dr. Rogers. May I ask if you are here for your health, sir!

Fred. [*Laughing.*] Not exactly, doctor!—There's nothing the matter with me!

Dr. Rogers. Ah, I see!—Merely on a pleasure trip, eh?

Fred. No,—I can't call it that either!— I'll be candid with you, doctor!—I am here to abduct one of your fair visitors!

Dr. Rogers. [*Astonished.*] Nonsense, sir!—Preposterous!

Fred. Not at all, doctor!—I am here to kidnap a lady.

Dr. Rogers. That would be the first time such a thing happened in Waukesha!—It's immoral, sir!

Fred. Not at all, doctor,—for the lady is my wife!

Dr. Rogers. Now, who has ever heard of a man wanting to kidnap his own wife!

Fred. Yes, I admit—it's not a daily occurrence!—Still circumstances alter cases! [*Goes to window R.*]

Dr. Rogers. [*Observing Fred closely,—aside.*] Very strange!

Fred. [*Looking through the window.*] There's the scoundrel now!

Dr. Rogers. [*Aside.*] And so excited! [*Joins Fred at the window.*] Whom do you refer to?

Fred. I'll strangle that rascal yet!

Dr. Rogers. [*Feeling Fred's pulse.*] Allow me!

Fred. [*Pulling his arm away,—angrily.*] Oh, don't bother me! [*Stares again out of the window.*]

Dr. Rogers. [*Aside.*] Yes, clearly a case of *non compos mentis!* [*Aloud.*] Mr. Harrison, you seem somewhat agitated! [**Fred** *turns towards him.*]

Fred. I have sufficient cause to be!

Dr. Rogers. You have perhaps been overworked lately!— What is your line of business, if I may inquire?

Fred. [*Forgetting himself.*] I'm in the dry goods—— [*Quickly correcting himself.*] I meant—I'm an artist,—a painter!

Dr. Rogers. What is your style?

Fred. I have preferred still-life till now,—but in the future— [*Looking again through the window.*] I am going to devote myself to battlepieces!

Dr. Rogers. [*Aside.*] There is no doubt!—His mind is upset! [*Points at his forehead.*]

Otto. [*Entering* C. D. *with another telegram.*]

Dr. Rogers. [*Aside to* **Otto.**] I say, Otto!—Is there a Mrs. Harrison stopping here?

Otto. Not vot I know of already, doctor!

Dr. Rogers. Yes, it's a clear case! [**Otto** *goes to Fred near window.*]

Otto. Here's another telegraph, Mr. Harrison!

Fred. [*Brusquely turning round, and tearing the telegram out of* **Otto's** *hand.*] Give it to me! [*Tears open the envelope and reads.*] "Your telegram a conundrum. What are you referring to?—Torrence."—Well,—if this doesn't beat the devil!

Dr. Rogers. Anything wrong, Mr. Harrison?

Fred. Anything wrong?—I should say so!—It seems that I've become a millionaire all of a sudden,—and that my partner has gone crazy!

Dr. Rogers. [*Aside.*] If there still were any doubt in my mind,—this hallucination about being a millionaire would confirm my suspicions!

Fred. [*To* **Otto.**] Is there such a thing as a long distance telephone in this place?

Otto. Yes, sir,—two blocks from here, round de corner!

Fred. I'll call up Torrence, and see if I can't get an explanation of all this! [*Takes up his hat and cane, and exit hastily* C. D.]

Otto. Vat is de matter mit dat man, doctor?

Dr. Rogers. Not a word of this to anybody, Otto!—It was a lucky thing that I made this discovery in time!

Otto. [*Curiously.*] Discovery, doctor?—What discovery?

Dr. Rogers. You must not mention this to a soul, Otto,—if you want to keep your place here!—The reputation of the hotel would be ruined for the entire season, if you did.—This man, Harrison, is suffering from delusions, and not in his right mind!

Otto. I thought so from the time he came, I bet you some, doctor!—He is been acting so queer und crazy-like already all de time!

Dr. Rogers. Be very careful and keep a strict watch over him! —If he should become violent, send for me at once!—I'll know how to quiet him, and get him out of the way, without any disturbance!

Otto. All right, doctor,—I'll watch him!

Dr. Rogers. We had better take some precautions, however! Who occupies the next room?

Otto. [*Pointing to door* L.] Mr. Growler is in dere, doctor!

Dr. Rogers. One of my most interesting patients!—We must protect him by all means! I'll see if he is in his room! [*Goes to door* L. *and knocks. A key is heard to turn in the lock, and the door is slightly opened.*]

Growler, [*Behind door* L.] Did you wish to see me, sir?

Dr. Rogers. [*To* **Otto.**] Move that sofa out of the way, Otto! [**Otto** *moves the sofa, which has been standing against the door, down stage, and somewhat removed from the wall.*]

Growler. [*Opening the door.*] Ah, is it you, doctor? I thought my neighbor wanted to see me!

Dr. Rogers. [*Mysteriously.*] Hush!—Step in here, sir!

Growler. What is the matter, doctor.

Dr. Rogers. I think it my duty to put you on your guard, Mr. Growler! Your neighbor, who occupies this room, is not quite safe!

Growler. What?—Still another——? [*Imitates the motions of a pickpocket.*]

Dr. Rogers. Oh, no;—he is not altogether in good health!

Growler. [*Frightened.*] Say, doctor,—is it catching?

Dr. Rogers. I mean—not quite right in his mind!

Growler. Good lord!—Oh, this is a lovely place to come to!— I knew room No. 13 would bring me bad luck!—I'll pack my trunk and leave here at once!

Dr. Rogers. There is no need to feel alarmed, Mr. Growler!— There is no danger whatsoever!—But I thought it better to warn you. in case you should happen to hear some unusual noise in this room!

Growler. If I stay here, I'll feel all the time as if I were sitting on a keg of gunpowder! [*The sound of an electric bell is heard far in the distance.* **Growler** *becomes frightened and grabs hold of the doctor's and* **Otto's** *arms, as if in great fear.*]

Otto. Of you please, Mr. Growler, turn me loose!—Dot bell rings for me already! [*Disengages himself and goes to* c. d.]

Dr. Rogers. Otto, you can lock the door on the outside;—I'll leave through Mr. Growler's room!

Otto. All right, doctor!

Dr. Rogers. And mind what I told you—not a word of all this to anyone, and keep a strict watch over him!

Otto. Of course, doctor,—I bet you some! [*Exit* c. d. *The key is heard to turn in the lock.*]

Growler. I had some conversation with this gentleman only a short time ago, and he appeared perfectly rational to me!

Dr. Rogers. [*Shrugging his shoulders.*] Oh, yes,—I can understand that easily enough!—They all have their lucid intervals!—They seldom last long though!

Growler. Well,— I'll have to change my room again!—They'll have to give me one as far removed from here as possible, or otherwise I'll go elsewhere!

Dr. Rogers. There's absolutely nothing to fear, I assure you, sir!—Besides the key is on your side of the door, and moreover there is a strong iron bolt to it, as you can see! [*Goes to door* L.]

Growler. [*Following him.*] Nevertheless I'll not feel comfortable during the night with a raving maniac next door to me!—He might batter in the door and try to kill me during my sleep! [*The doorknob of* c. d. *is tried from the outside. He becomes frightened.*] Great heavens, there he is back now! [*Runs off* *quickly* L., *following the doctor, closes and locks the door, while the* C. D. *is unlocked and opened. Enter* **Mildred** *and* **Jones.**]

Mildred. [*Looking round;—in a subdued tone.*] So,—here we are in the enemy's camp!—Luckily nobody saw us enter here!

Jones. [*In the same tone.*] I should say it was lucky, madam! You are promoting me to a candidacy in the state's prison, do you know?—Are you aware of the penalty for entering strange premises with malice aforethought, and with burglarious intentions?

Mildred. I am not, and I don't care a rap!—Ah, there is his satchel!

Jones. Strange that women have no respect for the majesty of the law!

Mildred. Stop your orations, and help me lift this satchel on the table!—It's too heavy for me alone! [*They place the satchel on the table.*] Now, out with your keys!—Quick!—Hurry up!

Jones. [*Pulls a bunch of keys out of his pocket;—reluctantly.*] I tell you, madam,—it's entirely unnecessary! Your niece has convinced herself completely that the gentleman was not her husband!

Mildred. I'm not as easily bamboozled as my niece!—I want ocular evidence, and I mean to have it!—He may have bought another suit of clothes, but he hasn't provided himself completely with new linen!—Come, on!—To your work!—I'll steady the satchel!

Jones. [*Groaning.*] Such stubbornness! [*Tries to open the satchel with one of the keys.*] It won't fit.

Mildred. [*Imperatively*] Then try the others!

Jones. [*Trying the other keys.*] No,—it's useless!—None of them will fit this lock!—Now, madam, that I have done your wish, I'm off! [*About to go up stage.*]

Mildred. [*Detaining him.*] No,—you're not!—I don't give in so easily!—I intend to come to the bottom of this!

Jones. Then you'll have to do so alone!—I am going to sneak! [*Goes up stage.*]

Mildred. You are, eh?—Very well!—If you get a cold reception from Miss Hebe, you can blame yourself!

Jones. [*Stops and returns slowly.*] Would you really have the heart to queer me with her?

Mildred. [*Imitating him.*] Yes, I would really have the heart to queer you with her!

Jones. [*Determinedly,*] Then I might as well take my chances with the district attorney! [*Takes up the satchel violently, and tries to open it by tearing the lid to pieces.*]

Mildred. [*Searching round.*] Oh,—here's a nail!—Wait a moment! [**Jones** *puts the satchel down.*] Bend this nail and try if you can not open the lock with it! [*Gives the nail to* **Jones.**]

Jones. [*With dignity.*] Madam, do you know that the law considers a bended nail in the light of a jimmy?

Mildred. I don't care whether its a jimmy or a johnny, so long you open the satchel with it!

Jones. And how do you expect me to bend it? With my teeth?

Mildred. [*Contemptuously.*] Weakling!—Baby!

Jones. You're not a baby by a long shot!—Here, you bend it! [*Offering her the nail.*]

Mildred. I'll get a hammer! [*Goes up stage and turns round. Dictatorially, stamping her foot.*] You stay here till I come back! [*Exit quickly* C. D.]

Jones.—She gives herself airs like a street-car conductor!—But what am I to do?—Lord, how those women can put on the thumbscrews!—Is marriage really worth all this bother?—Of course,—there are women—and women!—There's a great difference between them! —[*Placing his hand on his heart,—with mock pathos.*] Oh, Hebe!—Sweetest of all women,—angel placed in the highest niche of my affection,—will you ever come off your perch to put the thumbscrew on your hubby that is to be? [*Picks up the satchel again.* Fred *enters* C. D. *and watches him.*] Confound this satchel! If I could only open it!—I'll try my keys once more! [*Takes out his keys and trys to pick the lock.*] No,—it's useless! —None of them will fit!

Fred. [*Coming down stage,—cooly.*] Of course not!—That's a Yale lock!

Jones. [*Starts and drops the satchel.*] Great Scott!—I'm pinched!

Fred. Is this your regular occupation?

Jones. [*Pressing his hand on his heart.*] The first time in my life, I swear it!

Fred. [*Calmly, but sternly.*] Really?—Then I'll take care that it will also be the last time!

Jones. My dear sir,—you certainly do not imagine——

Fred. [*Stopping him*] I don't imagine anything!—I have seen with my own eyes,—that's sufficient, I think!

Jones. Please, listen to me. and I'll explain to you what got me into this damnable scrape! It's all on account of a woman!

Fred. Yes, I know!—you seem to be a red hot favorite with women! But I'll teach you a lesson!

Jones. My dear sir, you seem to bear me a grudge,—but I can assure you that I am innocent, and that Miss Green is at the bottom of it all!

Fred. You are only wasting your words with me!—You can tell all your troubles to the police later on!

Jones. [*Aghast.*] But, Mr. Harirson,—you'll surely not turn an innocent joke into——

Fred. Oh,—it's a beautiful joke to break into other people's rooms, and try to pick locks!

Jones. It's all because Miss Green thinks that you are somebody else in disguise, and she only wanted——

Fred. [*Again motioning him to stop.*] All your talk is useless! —Save your breath for the judge!

Jones. But I'll convince you that I'm speaking the truth!—I'll go after Miss Green and bring her here! [*Goes up stage.*]

Fred. [*Barring his way.*] Stop!—Not a step farther!

Jones. You won't let me prove my innocence?

Fred. You can do that to the police! [*Exit quickly* c. d. *and locks it behind him.*]

Jones. [*Vainly trying to burst open the door.*] Locked in!— The devil,—what a scrape!

Fred. [*Loudly off stage.*] Waiter,—call a policeman at once. Hurry up!

Otto. [*Off stage.*] All right, Mr. Harrison!

Jones. He has really sent for the police!—This is getting serious!—What if Hebe should see me under arrest?—What would she think of me?—They'll not catch me alive! [*Runs to window* R. *and looks down.*] Hm!—Three stories high!—I might break my neck if I jumped! [*Looks round the room.*] Is there no other way out of here?—Ah,—there's another door! [*Runs to door* L. *and turns the knob.*] Also locked!—Somebody may be in there! I'll see! [*Knocks loudly.*]

Hebe. [*Off stage* L.] Who's there?

Jones. Please open the door, quick!

Hebe. [*Unlocks and unbolts the door, and opens it.*]

Jones. Ah, it's you, Hebe!—How lucky!—You've saved me!

Hebe. Did they catch you at it?—Why didn't you go, when I told you to? I warned you!

Jones. I don't understand you any better now than I did before!—You are talking in riddles!—But for heaven's sake, let me get out of here through your room!—They locked me in here!

Hebe. Not a step nearer!—What other crime have you committed now?

Jones. Crime?—No crime at all!—Only Mr. Harrison caught me, while I was trying to pick the lock of his satchel!

Hebe. [*Startled.*] Oh, heaven!—And you call that no crime? —You ask me to let you escape?—I'll call the police!

Jones. Don't bother yourself!—That's already been done! [*Steps nearer to her.*] But every moment is precious!—Let me go!

Hebe. [*Wringing her hands.*] You misguided, unfortunate young man!

Jones. Save your compassion till later on, but let me pass now! [*Approaches* Hebe, *who has gradually left the door. He comes between the door and* Hebe, *who has become frightened, and has run behind the sofa.*]

Hebe. [*Tearfully and frightened.*] You wouldn't hurt me, would you?

Jones. The way is clear at last. I hold the door!

Hebe. [*Bursting out in tears.*] Oh, please,—don't hurt me, sir!

Jones. [*Becoming alarmed at seeing* Hebe *in tears, leaves the door, and comes down stage in front of the sofa.*] Hurt you, my darling? How could I?

Hebe. [*Frightened at seeing* Jones *approaching her.*] I'll call for help! [*Jumps back towards the door behind the sofa,* Jones *at the same time jumps towards the door in front of the sofa, and reaches it before* Hebe, *who jumps back behind the sofa.*]

Jones. Oh, no,—the door is mine!

Hebe. [*In despair.*] Oh,—what shall I do? [*Pulls out her purse.*] Here, sir,—take my purse!—There's only thirty-seven cents in it,—but here's my locket also! *Unfastens the locket from her neck.*] It's real gold.

Jones. [*Confounded.*] What?– Oh,—this is too much!

Hebe. No,— no!—You can have it all;—I'll put it here on the sofa,—only—please,—please,—leave me, sir!

Jones. Leave you?—Never—I swear it!

Hebe. [*Sinks down on her knees at the lower end of the sofa, and stretches out her hands imploringly towards him.*] Oh, sir,— have mercy!

Jones. [*Also falling on his knees near the other end of the sofa, and imitating her gestures.*] If you go down on your marrow bones, so will I!—It is I, Hebe, who implore your mercy!—Please, don't take me for a burglar or an assassin!—I wouldn't harm a hair on your dear hear!

Hebe. [*Pacified, and rising quickly.*] You are really not going to hurt me?

Jones. [*Still on his knees.*] I wouldn't hurt a cockroach!— Believe me,—no matter how much appearances are against me,— I'm as innocent as a new born lamb!

Hebe. Oh,—but I watched you in the garden myself, while you——— [*Imitates a pickpocket.*]

Jones. [*Jumping to his feet.*] You mean the business with that handkerchief?—Ask Mrs. Parker why I did that!—It was for your sake!

Hebe. Incomprehensible!—But what about the satchel?

Jones. Miss Green is to be blamed for that!—Ask her!—That was also done to obtain your good graces!

Hebe. I can't understand it at all!

Jones. There's no time now to explain everything!—Only this I will tell you,—that for your dear sake I would risk anything in my power!

Hebe. [*Hesitatingly.*] When I look into your eyes, I feel almost inclined to believe you!

Jones. My eyes are the mirrors of my soul!—You may believe and trust me!—My father always said that anybody might safely give a mortgage on my eyes!

Hebe. And you think I ought to risk it?

Jones. You will find it gilt edged security!

Hebe. I am inclined always to be cautious, sir!

Jones. We may never have a chance to meet again like this,—and a wise person grabs the opportunity whenever it offers itself! [*Approaches her gradually.*]

Hebe. Till now you certainly have not shown remarkable wisdom yourself!

Jones. Because I love you so foolishly!—Because you have bereft me of all my senses!

Hebe. In that case I will be lenient with you!

Jones. You're an angel!—And I freely forgive you your suspicions! [*Imitates a pickpocket.*] But all that is over now,—and before us lies a future of bliss and happiness!

Hebe. I depend entirely upon my uncle, sir!

Jones. I'll give him another massage treatment to-morrow, and ask for your hand at the same time! ·[*Takes her hand and brings it to his lips.*] Will you permit your mortgagor to pay his first interest? [*Kisses her hand.*] Now, as a matter of business may I ask for a receipt! [*Wipes his lips, and puckers them, as if expected to be kissed.—Several voices are heard behind c. d.*]

Hebe. [*Alarmed.*] I hear voices! [*The noise behind c. d. increases.*]

Fred. [*Off stage,—loudly.*] Here's the door sergeant!

Jones. [*Frightened.*] There's the police!—As usual,—when not wanted!

Hebe. Come quick,--through my uncle's room!

Jones. [*Grabbing Hebe's purse and locket from the sofa.*] Here's your thirty-seven cents, Hebe! [*Both exeunt quickly door L., Jones following Hebe. He closes and locks the door, while at the same time the c. d. is unlocked and opened, and Fred, Dr. Rogers, Sergeant Ripley, Otto and two insane asylum guards enter.*]

Fred. [*While entering, looking backward.*] Come in, gentlemen! [*Remains at the door ushering in the others.*]

Dr. Rogers. [*Aside to Sergeant Ripley.*] Give in to everything he says, sergeant!—The guards have their instructions.

Sergeant. [*Aside to Dr. Rogers.*] Very well, doctor!

Fred. [*After all have entered, turning round.*] Arrest that fellow——- [*Astonished at not seeing Jones.*] What the deuce has become of him? [*Calling.*] Mr. Jones!—Aha,--our man is hiding himself! [*Looks under the sofa.*]

Dr. Rogers. [*Aside to Sergeant Ripley.*] There's a specimen of his delusions! [*To the Guards.*] You have your instructions? [*The Guards nod.*]

Fred. [*Getting up again.*] The devil!

Sergeant. Can't you find him, sir?

Fred. I don't understand how he got out of here! [*Tries the doorknob of door L.*]

Dr. Rogers. That door is locked from the other side!

Fred. [*Opening the wardrobe.*] Empty!

Dr. Rogers and Sergeant Ripley. [*Looking at each other.*] Hm!—Hm!

Fred. [*Looking in the washstand.*] He couldn't very well hide in here!

Dr. Rogers. No, hardly!

Fred. [*Slightly irritated.*] Still I assure you, doctor, that I left him here,'and locked him in! [*Throws all the pillows and covers from the bed, and looks under it.*]

Sergeant. *While Fred ransacks the bed.*] Oh,—we'll take your word for that, sir!—Would you mind stating the facts once more?

Fred. [*Kicking his satchel out of the way impatiently.*] I knew the fellow in Chicago!—He sneaked into my house, under some pretext, in order to rob me of my life's happiness!

Dr. Rogers. Abominable!

Sergeant. Monstrous.

Fred. A little while ago I went to a telephone station to talk to my partner in Chicago, who wired me first that I had become a millionaire, and later on denied all knowledge of the fact!—I think he's suddenly gone crazy! [*The doctor and sergeant throw meaning glances at each other.*] Well,—somehow or another I couldn't connect with him, and when I came back to my room, I found this rascal trying to pick the lock of my satchel!—You know the rest, sergeant!

Sergeant. Yes, sir!—If we could only find our man!

Fed. It is your business to find him!—That's what you are on the police force for!

Sergeant. I'll do all I can, sir!—Will you be kind enough to come with me in the meantime?

Fred. I?—What for?

Dr. Rogers. You'd better go quietly along, Mr. Harrison?

Fred. Why should I? What do you want of me?

Sergeant. I want you to give us a full description of this fellow!

Fred. I have already done so, and told you all I knew about him!—His name is Jones, but that is probably an alias!—I can't leave here now, as I am expecting another wire from my partner! [*Sees* **Otto**, *who has been staring at him with wide open mouth.*] Why the devil are you staring at me in that way?

Otto. [*Frightened, stepping back.*] Och,—for nodding at all, sir!—Only joost so!

Fred. [*Following him, threateningly.*] What the dickens are you doing here anyhow?—What business have you got here?—I don't need you,—so get out of my room!

Otto. [*Trembling.*] Yes, sir!—All right, sir! [*Exit quickly* c. d.]

Dr. Rogers. [*Placing his hand on Fred's shoulder.*] There's no need to excite yourself like this, my dear sir!

Fred. And those two fellows! [*Pointing towards the guards.*] What are they doing in here?

Dr. Rogers. They are friends of mine!—They came with me! —Now, come,—control yourself!—Don't fly into a passion!—It's bad for you!

Fred. [*Furiously, stamping his foot.*] How in the devil's name do you expect me to control myself, when I see a lot of guys standing around here doing nothing, while this fellow, Jones, may be making his escape?

Growler. [*Sticking his head through door* L.] What's the meaning of all this noise in here?

Fred. Ah, my neighbor!—One moment, sir! [*Goes to door* L.] Did you see——?

Growler. [*Frightened.*] I've seen nothing! [*Slams the door.*]

Fred. Is this a conspiracy against me?

Dr. Rogers. Why, no,—Mr. Harrison!—We are all your friends here!

Sergeant. Certainly,—so long as you will quietly come along with us!

Fred. [*Angrily.*] The gods in their wrath must have turned you into a police sergeant!

Sergeant. Yes,—yes,—of course!—Quite right!

Fred. Sir,—are you trying to make a fool of me?

Growler. [*Again peeping through door* L.] Why don't you arrest that fellow?

Fred. That's all I want them to do!—Neighbor, I want your assistance! [*Goes to* L.]

Growler. Excuse me! [*Slams the door again.*]

Fred. [*Furiously, taking up his hat.*] This is more than I can stand! [*Slams the hat on his head.*]

Dr. Rogers. That's right!—Let us go, Mr. Harrison! [*Offers him his arm.*]

Fred. [*Impatiently.*] Ah,—what the dickens!—My name isn't Harrison!

Sergeant. Quite right, sir!—We know all about it!

Fred. [*Astonished.*] You know all about it?—How could you? —Nobody knows me here,—not even my own wife!

Sergeant. [*Trying to pacify him.*] Yes,—yes!—That'll be all right!

Dr. Rogers. [*Sternly, but without temper.*] But now it's our time to go!—Come along without any further disturbance, Mr. Harrison. [*Growler opens door* L. *again.*]

Fred. [*Slowly, restraining his passion.*] What are you driving at, doctor?

Jones. [*Enters* C. D., *smiling.*] Ah, good day, Mr. Harrison!— How are you, gentlemen!

Fred. [*Furiously.*] Ah, there he is now!—Seize that man!— Arrest him! [*At a sign of* **Dr. Rogers** *the guards take quickly*

hold of **Fred's** *arms and shoulders, so that he is unable to move.*]
What means this outrage?

Dr. Rogers. Keep cool, Mr. Harrison,—keep cool!

Growler. [*Stepping into the room.*] Hold him tight, boys!

Picture—Quick Curtain.

ACT IV.

SCENE: *The same setting as in Act II.—As the curtain rises enter* **Jones** R. U. E.

Jones. [*Looking at his watch, and afterwards up to the hotel windows.*] She promised to meet me this morning early in the garden!—Her curtain is raised!—Ah, here she comes now!

Hebe. [*Entering from hotel* L.] Good morning!

Jones. [*Going to meet her.*] My Hebe! [*Kisses her hand.*] Now,—let me quickly hear my fate!—What did your uncle say?

Hebe. [*Bends her head as if embarrassed.*]

Jones. Why are you silent?

Hebe. I haven't found the heart yet to speak to him!—I didn't think it would be such a difficult matter!—But last night I couldn't gather up courage enough to do it!—It has worried me so, that I have hardly been able to close my eyes!

Jones. While I dreamed sweet dreams of you all night!

Hebe. I hope you will forgive me for not speaking to him!— He was in such an awful bad humor!

Jones. His bad humor is like a continuous variety performance!--There's no intermission!—Only some of his turns are worse than the others!--If we wait till he gets an attack of good humor we'll both die old maids!

Hebe. Eh?

Jones. I mean—you will!

Hebe. But I have firmly made up my mind to speak to him during our breakfast this morning.—He likes to take it in the open air, and it usually brings him in a better temper, when he does.

Jones. If I were only sure that you would stick to your determination.

Hebe. [*Placing her hand on her heart.*] I promise you I will! Now, that I have seen you again, I'll be braver!

Jones. [*Placing his arm around her and drawing her towards him*] My darling!—And after you have made your confession, leave him to me!—I'll finish the siege, and take the old fortification by assault! [*Kisses her forehead.*]

Growler. [*Off stage* L., *loudly.*] Hebe! [*They separate quickly.*]

Hebe. [*Nervously.*] Run away!—Quick!

Jones. [*While running to* R. U. E.] Mind,—don't fail! [*Exit quickly* R. U. E.]

Growler. [*Entering from hotel* L.] So,—here you are!

Hebe. Yes, uncle,—I came out early in the garden to hear the birds sing!—It's so pretty! [*Affectionately placing her arm around him.*] How do you feel to-day uncle, dear? I believe you have had a good night's rest!

Growler. Not much!—What makes you think so?

Hebe. Because I could hear you snore all night!—Those partitions here are so thin!

Growler. Snore?—No such thing!—I never snore!—You may have heard me groan in pain, perhaps!

Hebe. I think you are looking ever so much better to-day!

Growler. You do? That would be extraordinary after all of yesterday's excitement and disturbance! [**Otto** *enters from hotel* L. *with a large tray on which are all the necessary breakfast ingredients. He sets the table* R., *and exit again in hotel.*]

Hebe. I wonder what has become of that poor Mr. Harrison!

Growler. Oh,—they've locked him up, of course!—That man was a dangerous lunatic!—We may congratulate ourselves that we got rid of him! [*They go to table* R. *and sit down for their breakfast.*] Pour out my coffee, my dear!

Hebe. [*Serving him.*] Shall I get you a footstool, uncle?

Growler. No,—never mind!—It doesn't seem damp here!

Hebe. Or do you want your shawl?

Growler. [*Gazing at her fixedly.*] Hebe,—you seem extraordinarily anxious about me to-day!

Hebe. I am always anxious for your health, dear!—Don't you always take care of me?—It's the least return I can make for your kindness to me!—And who knows what a short time fate may leave us together!

Growler. [*Half rising in fear.*] Do you think I am nearing my end? Do I look that bad?

Hebe. Oh, no,—uncle,—I didn't mean it that way at all!

Growler. [*Sitting down again.*] How then?

Hebe. Circumstances might arise which would compel me to leave you!

Growler. [*Dropping a piece of toast.*] What are you talking about?

Hebe. [*Handing him another piece of toast.*] Go ahead with your breakfast, uncle,—and I'll explain to you what I mean!—You know, dear,—that I love you dearly, for you have always been so good to me!—But there might come somebody else some day, whom I would be bound to love still more!

Growler. Here,—don't you commence any nonsense of that kind, do you hear!

Hebe. It is written that a wife must leave her father and mother!

Growler. [*Angrily.*] Yes,—that's all right,—but it doesn't mention a word about the uncle!—For the Lord's sake, Hebe,—you are not thinking of getting married!—A mere slip of a girl like you!

Hebe. [*With some effort.*] I hate to give you pain, uncle,—but I must admit that I am thinking of it most seriously!

Growler. [*Rising.*] You have completely spoiled my appetite for breakfast! ·

Hebe. [*Rising quickly,—going towards him; carressingly.*] Please, uncle do not feel annoyed!—It won't be necessary for me to leave you altogether!—I will always take care of you!—You might come and live with us!

Growler. [*Perplexed*] With us?—Then the somebody has already come, eh?

Hebe. [*Meekly.*] Yes, uncle,—he has! [*Patting him on the cheeks affectionately.*]

Growler. [*Annoyed, pushing her hand away.*] Oh,—stop your love pats!—You don't mean them anyway!—You'd better bottle up your affection for him!—You might just as well finish me off at a stroke!—I hate to be tortured to death slowly!—Who is he?—Where is he?

Hebe. [*Embarrassed, turning down her eyes.*] That's just the thing, uncle!

Growler. I know all about the thing!—I want to know who the person is!—Come,—out with it!

Hebe. It will surprise you so, when he comes to speak to you!

Growler. Surprise?—I hate surprises!—They're bad for the nerves!

Hebe. I mean when you see who it is!

Growler. See here,—I don't like to be guessing conundrums! —Is he here in Waukesha?

Hebe. [*Nods.*] That is a proof of his love for me, uncle!—He has followed me here!

Growler. Is that all the occupation he has, to go gallivanting all over the country after girls?

Hebe. I regarded him at first with suspicion,—but you have only to look well into his eyes to know that you may trust him.

Growler. I'll prefer to look into his pocketbook!

Hebe. Oh,—I didn't think of such a thing!

Growler. And where is this individual?

Hebe. [*Caressingly.*] You'll soon see him, uncle! [*Exit quickly L. 2. E. behind arbor.*]

Growler. [*Calling after her.*] Hebe,—come back here! [*Enter* **Otto** *from hotel* L.]

Otto. [*Pointing to the breakfast table.*] Can I take dose dings avay already, sir?

Growler. [*Angrily.*] No!—Get out! [*Goes back to the table.*]

Otto. [*Frightened.*] Och,—oxcuse me, sir! [*Exit back in hotel* L. *while* **Growler** *sits down.*]

Growler. [*Grumbling.*] To torture me like this, and not even to mention his name! It's unpardonable!—How does she expect me to enjoy my breakfast!

Jones. [*Entering, unperceived by* **Growler** R. U. E.] The preliminary attack has been successful,—the uncle is alone! [*Approaching and greeting him.*] Good morning Mr. Growler!

Growler. [*Jumping up.*] There's that pickpocket! [*Places his hand on his pockets.*] What do you want?

Jones. I've come to ask you if you would like to take another massage treatment!

Growler. No, sir!—No, sir!—I've had all the massage I want! —If you think I'm a piece of dough that wants kneading, you're mistaken!

Jones. You're losing a splendid opportunity to get well, sir!

Growler. [*Motioning him away.*] I haven't lost the opportunity to lose my pocketbook at least!

Jones. [*Taking a pocketbook from his pocket.*] Is this the one, sir?

Growler. Of course, it is!

Jones. One of the waiters found it here on the ground yesterday,—and didn't know to whom it belonged!—I'm glad to be able to return your property to you!

Growler. [*Taking the pocketbook,—aside.*] Because there was no money in it! [*Aloud.*] Thanks! [*Retreats a few steps from* **Jones.**]

Jones. [*Following him unconcernedly.*] And now,—I would like to speak a few words with you in my own behalf!

Growler. Keep away from me, if you please!

Jones. Why,—you don't think that I would give you a treatment against your will?

Growler. I'll feel obliged to you if you'll keep your distance!

Jones. Mr. Growler,—I wish to speak to you on a delicate subject,—which I do not care to cry over the housetops!—Besides you are slightly hard of hearing!

Growler. And you seem somewhat dull of comprehension!—Haven't I made it sufficiently plain that I do not wish to speak to you?

Jones. [*Aside.*] In bad humor, as usual!

Growler. Good day, sir!

Jones. [*Shrugging his shoulders.*] I'll have to watch for a more favorable opportunity! [*Aloud.*] Good morning, sir! [*Exit behind arbor* L. 2 E.]

Growler. [*Only nods his head.*] I wonder if I'll ever get a chance to eat my breakfast to-day! [*Sits down again at the table.*]

Harrison. [*Entering from* R. U. E., *looking at his watch.*] Well, —I've taken my morning's constitutional!—Glad it's over! [*To* **Growler.**] Good morning, sir!

Growler. [*Annoyed.*] Morning!

Harrison. You seem to be enjoying your breakfast!

Growler. No, sir!—It's almost choking me!

Harrison. [*Taking a seat opposite* **Growler**,— *laughing.*] So you said last night at dinner, but still you seemed to stow away a hearty meal!—I wish I could do likewise,— but I'm here to reduce myself! [*Slapping his stomach.*] It's like torture to me, I tell you!—My only pleasure in life is to eat and drink well!—And as I have neither kith nor kin——

Growler. You may be glad of it!—Marriage is all humbug!

Harrison. Yes,— I've often thought so!—Still, when a man is worth about a million and a half like myself——

Growler. [*Starts.*] A million and a——

Harrison. Ah!—We won't mention the half!—Otherwise they'll want to increase my taxes still more!—I wonder really what they have taxed me at!—My friend, Will Humphrey, promised to wire me before I left Chicago, but I haven't heard from him as yet! [*Looking round.*] What's become of your niece?

Growler. She went for a walk!

Harrison. Seems to be a charming girl, do you know!

Growler. [*Coolly.*] You think so?

Harrison. I certainly do!—She's made quite an impression on me!—So refined and graceful,—so attractive and ladylike!

Growler. Hm!

Harrison. So,—she's lost her parents, and is living with you eh?

Growler. How do you know this, sir?

Harrison. She's told me so!

Growler. [*Aside.*] Great heaven,—can this be the—— [*Gazes at* **Harrison** *as if dumbfounded.*]

Harrison. What did you say?

Growler. Nothing, sir.—nothing at all!

Harrison. I suppose it would be quite a sacrifice if you should have to give her up some day!

Growler. We haven't got as far as that yet, I hope!

Harrison. [*Playfully shaking his finger at him.*] Oh,—I don't know!—You may have to bite the sour apple, sooner than you think!

Growler. [*Excitedly.*] What's the use of all this subterfuge? Why don't you come out plainly, and say that you want my Hebe?

Harrison. [*Astonished.*] I?

Growler. Yes, you!—You want to marry her,—that's quite clear to me!

Harrison. Such an idea never entered my head, sir!

Growler. Then I wish you wouldn't put any more foolish notions into her head!

Harrison. I never did such a thing!

Growler. You certainly gave her to understand that you had serious intentions, sir!

Harrison. [*Rising.*] Excuse me, sir,— you are wrong!

Growler. [*Also rising,—gesticulating across the table towards Harrison.*] You have not behaved yourself like a gentleman, sir!

Harrison. What the deuce!—Yesterday at the spring I gave her a few roses, and paid her some compliments!—Does that mean that I want to marry her?

Growler. [*Knocking on the table.*] At least you made my niece understand that much, sir!

Harrison. Then the sooner you talk that idea out of your niece's head, the better it will be, sir!

Growler. That's your business!—It's you who have insulted her!—You owe her an explanation, sir!

Harrison. No, thanks!—I don't want to run any more risks at being misunderstood!

Growler. Sir, it is your duty,—and if you are a gentleman, you will apologise to her.

Harrison. You may take me for a fool, sir,—but you'll find that I'm not so easily taken in!—Your blackmailing scheme won't work with me!—You can get rid of your niece to somebody else, but not to me. [*Going towards hotel* L.—*Aside.*] Bah,—it's a confidence game! [*Exit in hotel* L.]

Growler. [*Astonished, placing his arms akimbo.*] Well,—I never!—Does that stuffed chimpanzee imagine that I want to get rid of my Hebe?—But wait,—I'll have a few words to say to her when she comes back! [*Sits down again at his breakfast.*]

Cora. [*Entering* R. U. E., *dressed extravagantly like a servant in her Sunday clothes.*] I think this must be the place! [*Sees* Growler.] There's a gentleman;—I'll ask him! [*Taps Growler on the shoulder.*] I say, mister!

Growler. [*Startled.*] Well,—what do you want?

Cora. Can you tell me if this is the Park Hotel?

Growler. [*Annoyed.*] Can't you read that sign over there?

Cora. [*Looks at the sign over entrance of hotel.*] Oh, yes.—I didn't see it before!—Thank you for the information, sir!

Growler. [*Eating.*] Don't mention it! [*Enter Otto from hotel* L., *and comes down the steps.*]

Cora. [*To Otto.*] Do you belong here, sir?

Otto. [*Extravagantly polite.*] Yes, Miss!—What can I do for you already yet?

Cora. I've just come in on the train!—My missus, Mrs. Parker, is stopping here!

Otto. Oh, yes!—Oh, yes! No. 32!—She has gone already for a morning walk mit No. 34,—Miss Green!

Cora. And what is the number of the master's room?

Otto. The master?—What master?

Cora. [*Aside.*] I nearly forgot myself!—Mr. Torrence told me to be careful! [*Aloud.*] Isn't there a Mr. Harrison stopping here?

Otto. Two Mr. Harrisons, I bet you some!—One is fat and jolly.——

Cora. Mine is thin and cranky!

Otto. [*Aside.*] Och, jimminy! [*Aloud, somewhat confused.*] Yah,—dat one is not stopping here already any more!

Cora. What?—Where is he gone?

Otto. Och, Miss,—dat vas a secret, vat I cannot tell you already now!—Mrs. Parker vas also asking me dis morning!

Cora. [*Anxiously.*] But it is absolutely necessary that I should see him!

Otto. Yah,—dat may be, but I cannot tell you so!—Vot do you vant to see him apout, Miss?

Cora. [*Snappishly.*] Is that any of your business?

Otto. Och, no,—of course not!—I only ask just so!—But nobody can see him yet for some time, I bet you some!—He vas dangerous!

Cora. [*Anxiously.*] What do you mean?

Otto. Och,—noddings!—I cannot tell you!—But here comes Mrs. Parker, already!—You better ask her! [*Exit quickly in hotel* L. *Enter* **Vivian** *and* **Mildred** R. U. E.]

Vivian. [*Frightened at seeing* Cora.] Great Heaven!

Growler. [*Startled, jumps up.*] Oh, Lord! [*Sinks back in his chair.*]

Vivian and Mildred. [*Together.*] Cora!

Cora. Yes,—it's me, ma'am!—Don't be frightened!

Vivian. What has happened at home?

Cora. Nothing at all, ma'am!—I came to find out what is the matter here!—Mr. Torrence sent me!—He got several telegrams from the master yesterday, to which he could not make head nor tail!—They're so busy at the office that he couldn't come himself, nor spare anyone else, and so he sent me.—Where is Mr. Parker, ma'am?

Vivian. I wish I could tell you!—We have been looking for him everywhere!—I feel as if I'm going out of my mind!—Heaven only knows what may have happened to him!

Mildred. Come, come, Vivian! Have a little common sense!—You can't lose a man like a hair-pin!—This sudden disappearance is certainly another one of his tricks!

Vivian. No, no, aunt!—He's doing it to torture and punish me!—If you only knew how shamefully I treated him yesterday! [*Goes up stage with* **Mildred** *conversing.*]

Cora. [*Shrugging her shoulders.*] Now I'm just as wise as when I came!

Jones. [*Entering* L. 2 E., *and approaching* Growler *from behind.*] I'll try my luck once more! [*Taps* Growler *on the shoulder.*] Mr. Growler!

Growler. [*Shrinking together in fear, and slowly turning towards* Jones.] Ah!– What,–you again!

Jones. I've merely come to ask if after your breakfast you feel somewhat kindlier disposed!

Growler. [*Grumbling.*] No, on the contrary!

Vivian. [*Seeing* Jones.] Ah,–there is Mr. Jones!

Jones. [*Greeting the ladies.*] Ladies!–Good morning! [*Goes towards them.*]

Cora. [*Surprised at seeing* Jones.] What,–that man here too!

Vivian. Will you give us your assistance?–My husband has completely disappeared since yesterday!

Jones. [*Dumbfounded.*] What?– Then it was he after all?

Vivian. Do you know what has become of him?

Jones. Yes,–I do know,--I am sorry to say!

Vivian. [*Horrified.*] Sorry to say?–Heaven, what has happened to him?

Jones. [*Confused.*] Well,——hm!

Mildred. Come,–don't keep her in any unnecessary suspense! —Tell us!

Jones. There's absolutely no need to excite yourselves, ladies! –He is in no danger whatsoever, and well taken care of!

Cora. I'll bet the master's being locked up!

Jones. I'll go after him and bring him back with me here alive and well in less than five minutes!

Vivian. [*Quickly.*] I'll go with you!

Jones. Pardon me, madam,–but that would hardly do!–His present abode is scarcely fit to receive ladies!–I'll be back in no time! [*Exit* R. U. E.]

Mildred. Do you understand anything of all this, Vivian?

Vivian. I don't, aunt,–and I don't care to!–So long as I get my Fred back! [*They go up stage looking off after* Jones, *and walk off slowly* R. U. E.]

Cora. This is a case of lost, strayed, or stolen! [*Exit* R. U. E.]

Hebe. [*Entering* L. 2 E. *and coming behind* Growler, *she places her hand on his shoulder.*] Uncle, dear!

Growler. [*Jumping up again, startled.*] Ah!–Why are you all trying to scare the life out of me?

Hebe. Excuse me, uncle,–I didn't mean to!–Has he been here?

Growler. Of course, he has! [*Throws down his napkin and leaves the table.*]

Hebe. Well——and——

Growler. Hebe,—I can stand a good deal of foolishness from you,—but I never thought you could have been so downright stupid!

Hebe. Stupid?

Growler. You put me in a most awkward position!—But you are all alike!—No sooner does a man pay you a few silly compliments, but you imagine that he can no longer live without you!

Hebe. Uncle, I am positive he can not live without me!—What impression did he make on you?

Growler. I don't see how he could possibly have made an impression on you!—Of course,—he's worth a million and a half——

Hebe. He never told me that,—and besides—it's of no consequence!

Growler. Then I cannot understand it at all!—You told me to look into his eyes, eh?—I did!—He's wall-eyed,—he's got eyes like a pig!

Hebe. Oh, uncle!

Growler. But that's neither here nor there!—There's no accounting for tastes! He may be a perfect Adonis in your eyes!—The only thing is that the man hasn't the slightest idea of getting married!

Hebe. [*With more emphasis.*] Oh,—uncle!

Growler. Yes,—oh, uncle!—He was perfectly plain in that respect!

Hebe. You've simply misunderstood him!

Growler. Have I?—I may be slightly hard of hearing, but when a man becomes so insulting as he did,—there can hardly be a question of misunderstanding.

Hebe. [*Perplexed.*] What?—Can he have made game of me? Oh, it's impossible!—But if he has,—we ought not to let it pass like this!

Growler. I don't intend to,—we'll punish him with our utter contempt!

Hebe. No, no,—that won't be sufficient!—You will have to call him to account, uncle!

Growler. I call him to an account?—An invalid like me?—Why,—the fellow is as strong as an ox!

Hebe. [*Excitedly.*] I will have satisfaction!

Growler. For heaven's sake don't let us have any fuss!—What if other people should hear of this!

Hebe. There is nothing I have to be ashamed of!—I want everybody here to know it, so he'll be ashamed to stay!

Growler. Oblige me with one thing, and create no scandal!—Pay no more attention to him than if he didn't exist!—Bah! [*Enter* **Harrison** *from hotel* L. *with a newspaper.*—**Growler** *passes him, not noticing him.—On the top of the steps he turns round and throws a contemptuous glance towards* **Harrison.**] Bah!

[*Exit in hotel.* **Harrison** *looks after him with an amused smile, shrugs his shoulders, sits down* R. *and commences to read.*]

Hebe. [*Aside.*] No,—I won't stand it!—There's that stout gentleman who was so kind to me yesterday!—I think he will take my part! [*To* Harrison.] Excuse me, Mr. Harrison, if I disturb you!

Harrison. [*Rising,—aside.*] Now she's coming to the attack herself!

Hebe. Oh,—please, keep your seat, sir!

Harrison. No,—thanks!

Hebe. Would you kindly spare me one minute?

Harrison. Pardon me,—but I have a splitting headache! [*Is about to leave.*]

Hebe. And my heart is almost breaking!

Harrison. Why can't you leave an old fellow like myself alone?

Hebe. Oh, sir,—you were so kind and attentive to me yesterday, that——

Harrison. I promise you that it won't occur again!—Your uncle told me what foolish nonsense you've got into your head!

Hebe. Then you know how miserable I must feel!—Oh, please, won't you be my protector? [*She places her hand confidingly on his arm.*]

Harrison. [*Evading her.*] It's a great honor, no doubt,—but I would rather not!—You had better look for someone else!

Hebe. But can't you feel,—can't you understand what an agony it must be to me,—to find myself so terribly mistaken?

Harrison. If you please, miss,—don't try to play on my feelings!—It's absolutely useless, I tell you!

Hebe. Not a single soul seems to have compassion on me! [*Exit weeping* R. 2.E.]

Harrison. [*Dryly.*] I must admit that the old man has found an apt pupil in his niece,—but I've been through the mill too often to be caught by any game of this kind! [*Exit in hotel* L.]

Vivian. [*Entering* R. U. E., *followed by* **Mildred** *and* **Cora.**—*Joyfully.*] Oh, aunt,—there they come!

Mildred. [*Coolly.*] Now, Vivian,—there's no need to make an exhibition of yourself! [*Leads her down stage.*]

Vivian. Oh, aunt,—my heart is almost bursting!

Cora. [*Up stage looking off* R.] The master looks as if he had had the starch taken out of him! [*Enter* Jones *and* Fred R. U. E., *remaining up stage.*]

Jones. [*Smiling.*] Here, ladies,—I restore to you the prodigal husband!—I'll be discreet and vamoose! [*Exit behind hotel* L. U. E. Fred *comes slowly down stage* C., *with downcast eyes.* Cora *follows him on his* R., *in utter amazement.*]

Vivian. Goodness gracious,—what has come over him?

Cora. He looks all done up, ma'am!

Vivian. [*Piqued.*] Cora,—go inside, and let them give you some breakfast!

Cora. Yes, ma'am,—but I would like to know——

Vivian. Go inside at once, I tell you!

Cora. All right, ma'am! [*Goes to hotel* L.—*Aside.*] I'm just dying to find out all about it!—What a pity! [*Exit in hotel* L.]

Vivian. [*Approaching* Fred.] Fred!

Fred. [*Without lifting his eyes,—meekly.*] Vivy!

Vivian. For the love of heaven,—tell me where you have been?

Fred. [*As above.*] Please,—don't ask me!

Mildred. But we want to know all about it!

Fred. [*Pointing at* Mildred.] You are to blame for it all!

Mildred. Oh, yes,—of course!—That doesn't astonish me!

Vivian. Where were you all night?

Fred. I would rather not speak of it!

Mildred. We are only among ourselves here!

Vivian. [*Coaxingly.*] Please,—tell us, Fred!

Fred. [*Groaning.*] I suppose I'll have to tell you,—but swear that you will never mention it to a living soul,—especially not to Torrence!

Mildred. Never a word of it!

Fred. [*Hesitatingly,—after a short pause.*] No,—I haven't got the heart to tell you!—Only this I must say to you, Vivian,—that after I found myself alone——

Vivian. [*Sympathetically.*] All alone, dear?

Fred. [*Sighing.*] Yes,—all alone,——I made up my mind never to let my temper get the better of me again!

Vivian. If you do that, Fred,—I'll promise you never to contradict you again! [Mildred *shrugs her shoulders in derision.*]

Fred. [*Affectionately.*] Sweetheart!

Vivian. My darling!

Fred. My own dearest wife!

Mildred. [*Aside.*] Now, wouldn't that make anyone sick?

Fred. In reality we have always loved each other most dearly,—haven't we, Vivy?

Vivian. I've always loved you better than you did me, dear!

Fred. Oh, no,—my angel!

Vivian. Oh, yes,—for you mistrusted me!—You had no faith in me, so aunt Mildred told me!

Fred. [*Turning towards* Mildred.] Very much obliged to you!

Mildred. Well,—wasn't I right?—Didn't you come here to play the spy on her?

Vivian. [*Throwing her arms around him.*] You will never do so again, will you, darling?

Fred. What worried me the most was to see the little attention aunt Mildred paid to you!

Mildred. [*Sarcastically.*] Oh, yes,—of course!—It's always aunt Mildred.

Vivian. Anyhow your anxiety was a proof of your affection for me, and I forgive you also what you said to aunt Mildred about me!

Fred. [*Turning towards* **Mildred,**—*angrily.*] What did I say to her?

Vivian. That my good looks were only a source of bother to you!

Fred. [*Looking angrily towards* **Mildred.**] What do you want to twist my words round like that for? [*To* **Vivian.**] All I meant to say was that you were far too pretty for me!

Vivian. Oh,—that sounds differently! [*Reproachfully to* **Mildred.**] Oh, aunt,—how could you?

Mildred. [*Opening her parasol with a snap,—disgusted.*] Good morning. [*Exit* R. U. E.]

Fred. [*Taking a deep breath.*] At last she's left us alone! [*Leads* **Vivian** *to arbor* L., *sits down, pulls her beside him, and kisses her.*]

Vivian. [*Throwing her arms around him.*] My darling, at last I've got you again!

Cora. [*Without hat from hotel* L.] I've had my breakfast, ma'am! [**Vivian** *jumps up quickly.*]

Fred. [*Annoyed.*] Then go back and have another one on me!

Cora. [*Astonished.*] All right, sir! [*Exit again in hotel* L., *looking back at the arbor.*]

Vivian. [*Seating herself again.*] Haven't we been awfully foolish, dear,—to make our lives miserable with our petty quarrels?

Fred. Do you know what I have been thinking about in the solitude of my———hm!———of my apartment?—If we ever should quarrel again———

Vivian. [*Quickly interrupting him.*] Oh,—but that will never happen any more!

Fred. Well,—let's hope not,—but still it might!

Vivian. No,—I've firmly made up my mind!—If it does,—it would entirely be your fault!

Fred. We'll see!—But what I meant to say is—let us start a sort of contribution box.—Whoever begins to quarrel will have to pay a fine!

Vivian. [*Quickly.*] Five dollars.

Fred. [*Hesitatingly.*] Well,—that's rather high!

Vivian. See,—you're afraid!

Fred. [*Affectionately.*] Only for your sake, darling!—Let's make it fifty cents!

Vivian. All right then!

Fred. But don't forget about it before you get back to Chicago!

Vivian. Why,—are you not going to stay here?—Then I'll go back on the same train with you!

Fred. No, dear,—you'd better stay here and enjoy yourself for a while!—I want to prove to you that I have absolute confidence in you!

Vivian. And I want to prove my love to you by returning home with you!

Fred. No, no,—you must do as I tell you! [*Vivian turns her head away as if displeased.* **Fred** *takes her by the shoulders, and gently makes her face him again.*] Your husband ought to know what should be done!

Vivian. Indeed?—And why shouldn't the wife? [*Rises in bad humor.*] I suppose you know better because you have ten per cent more brain than I!

Fred. [*Stretching out his hand towards her.*] Vivian, fifty cents fine, please!

Vivian. I?—Excuse me!—It's you who owe a fine!

Fred. That's a peculiar logic!

Vivian. When you tease and annoy me, it's certainly you who should pay a fine!

Fred. You'll have to wait a long time before I do!

Vivian. Oh,—of course!—I expected that!—Whatever you say —is right!—You are the lord and master!—Whatever you wish is law!—All I have to do is to obey!—You command that I shall stay,—very well—I'll do so!—You can go alone!—But never tell me again that it costs you pain to leave me!—It's quite clear now that you let me go from you " with the greatest pleasure."

Fred. [*Jumping up, angrily hitting the table.*] You are trying to exasperate me again!—You will really drive me insane yet!

Mildred. [*Entering* R. U. E.] Ah,—at it again, beloved children? —I thought it wouldn't take long!

Vivian. Oh, aunt,—protect me from his insults!

Fred. [*On the other side of her.*] See here, aunt Mildred,— you're a person of good, common sense!

Mildred. What?—All of a sudden?

Vivian. [*Pulling* **Mildred** *away.*] Don't listen to him, aunt!

Mildred. [*Pacifying her.*] No, no!

Fred. Aunt,—she is behaving herself again like a baby!

Mildred. [*Same bus.*] Yes, yes!

Vivian. Should I stand such a treatment as this?

Mildred. Certainly not!

Fred. That settles it!—I'll get my satchel and go! [*Runs towards hotel* L.]

Vivian. You see,—that's all he wanted! [**Fred** *turns round on the steps, throws up his hands in anger, and exit in hotel.*] Any pretext to get rid of me!

Mildred. That doesn't astonish me at all!

Vivian. What?

Mildred. I knew it had to come to this!—When two married people cannot get along together, the best thing they can do is to separate!

Vivian. [*Horrified.*] Auntie, do you really mean that?

Mildred. Most decidedly!—You might be living in an earthly paradise, if you wanted to!—But you don't seem to know the way towards it!

Vivian. If you know the way, aunt Mildred,—then for pity sake show it to me!

Mildred. Then, in the first place,—you'll have to learn to control your temper,—and to give in—even when you think your husband is wrong!

Vivian. [*Crosses her arms in front of her, walks a few times quickly up and down in meditation and suddenly halts in front of Mildred.*] Aunt!

Mildred. Well?

Vivian. [*Pulls out her purse.*] Come with me!—I know what to do now! [*Drags her aunt quickly off in hotel* L. *Enter* **Jones** *from behind hotel* L., *and* **Hebe** *from* R. 2 E.]

Jones. Ah, Hebe,—at last I find you!

Hebe. [*Coolly.*] How dare you still to address me, sir?

Jones. [*Astonished.*] Why, Hebe,—what means this?

Hebe. I forbid you to use my name, or address me in any form whatsoever!—We are total strangers, sir!

Jones. Well,—I'll sink into the ground!

Hebe. Go ahead and sink!—I won't dig you up again!—If there's not a man here who has courage enough to tell you the truth, I'll do so myself!—Your million and a half doesn't give you the right to insult unprotected women!

Jones. My million and a half?—Good lord!

Hebe. If you were to throw them at my feet, I——

Jones. I would do so with the greatest pleasure, if I only had them!

Hebe. Your money is absolutely nothing to me!

Jones. All right!—Then we'll drop the financial topic, and speak of——

Hebe. I won't speak another word to you!—Go away, and leave me! [*About to cross to the hotel.*]

Jones. [*Barring her passage.*] No,—I'll stay here, till I've had an explanation of all this!

Hebe. Very well,—you stay,—then I'll go! [*Crossing to* L. *and turning round,—indignantly.*] You—you hypocrite! [*Exit quickly* L. 2 E.—**Jones** *remains looking after her in amazement.—Enter* **Fred** *from hotel* L. *with satchel and ulster, followed by* **Otto** *with a bill.*]

Jones. What evil spirit is at work here! [**Fred** *bumps against him with his satchel.*—**Jones** *turns towards him.*] Excuse me, sir!

Otto. It's too bad you vant to leave us already, Mr. Parker!

Fred. Is it any of your business?

Otto. Och, no!—You forget your bill, sir! [*Presents the bill.*]

Fred. [*Takes the bill, looks it over,—then up to the hotel,—suddenly.*] Tell my wife to pay it!

Otto. All right, sir! [*Exit quickly in hotel* L.]

Fred. Now she'll see that I'm in earnest!

Jones. My dear Mr. Parker, you have plenty of time before the next train!—I wish you would do me the favor to speak a good word for me to Mr. Growler, before you leave!—For some reason or another the old bear won't let me come near him!—You know —one good turn deserves another!

Fred. [*Puts down his satchel and throws his ulster upon it.*] Why, my dear sir,—with the greatest pleasure!—If it hadn't been for you, I might still be listening to the tale of woe of Julius Cæsar, my next door neighbor!

Jones. I can't imagine what he has been telling his niece about me,—but I'm certainly in her black books just now!

Fred. Leave it to me.—I'll square matters for you!

Jones. I'll be your life long debtor if you do!—Now to try and speak to Hebe once more! [*Exit quickly* L. 2 E.]

Fred. Glad I found an excuse for delay! [**Cora** *enters from hotel* L., *and picks up the satchel without speaking.*] What are you doing Cora?

Cora. I'm going to take your satchel up stairs again, sir! The Missus says you're not going to leave anyhow!

Fred. She does, eh?—Well she's mistaken!—I am going to leave by the next train!—I only want to see Mr. Growler for a moment before I go!

Cora. Well,—what am I to do now?

Fred. Go and have some breakfast! [*Exit in hotel* L.]

Cora. [*Holding her sides.*] No, thanks,—I couldn't eat another morsel!—Now I don't know what the missus wants, and I don't know what the master wants!—I don't think they know what they want themselves!

Otto. [*From hotel* L., *remains on the steps.*] Well, Miss,—und how do you like it already in Waukesha?—Pretty good place, I bet you some,—don't it?

Cora. Ah, what!—They want to feed people to death here!

Otto. [*Astonished.*] Vell, vell,—dot's de first dime sooch a complaint has been made here already! [*They walk off conversing behind hotel* L. U. E.]

Growler. [*Entering slowly from hotel.*] Now, I wonder where that girl is keeping herself! [*Enter* **Fred** *from hotel. He taps* **Growler** *on the shoulder. The latter starts, looks round, sees* **Fred**, *and shrinks together with fear.*] Ah! [*He is about to make his escape, but is detained by* **Fred**, *who grabs him by the hand.*]

Fred. Don't run away!—I only want one word with you!

Growler. [*Aside.*] It's always best to humor those people!

Fred. What have you got against Mr. Jones?

Growler. He doesn't concern me in the least, sir!

Fred. Now,—just for the sake of argument—imagine that I am Jones!

Growler. [*Aside.*] There he goes again with his delusions!

Fred. I am in comfortable circumstances and able to support a wife. There's a clear profit of two hundred per cent in the drug business —I come to Chicago and meet a certain young lady! [*Gesticulates lively.*] You understand, eh?—It's a question of love at first sight!—The only girl for me in the whole world!— Just a plain American girl is good enough for me,—and all that sort of thing!—The question is for you to say " Yes " or " No! "— Am I clear, uncle, eh? [*Digs him in the ribs.*]

Growler. Perfectly! [*Aside.*] He might as well be talking Swedish to me!

Fred. Now,—quick!—Your answer!

Growler. Quick?—Excuse me,—I've just taken a bath, and feel somewhat chilly!—I want to go and get my overcoat! [*Is about to leave.*]

Fred. [*Detaining him, and offering him his ulster.*] Here put on my coat,—that will keep you warm!

Growler. [*Aside,—nervously.*] If I could only get away from here!

Fred. [*Holds up the ulster for* **Growler** *to put it on.*] Come on!—Hurry up! [*Assists* **Growler** *in putting on the ulster, which is much too large for him.*] Now, button it up in front.

Growler. [*Aside.*] This thing feels like a straight jacket!— It's impossible to escape in it!

Fred. Now, you're warm and comfortable!—Give me your answer!

Growler. Excuse me,—but what did you ask me?

Fred. What the devil!—Is your memory so short?

Growler. [*Anxiously.*] Please, don't get excited!

Fred. Well,—will you give her to Jones—yes or no?

Growler. Who?

Fred. I'll be blowed!—Your niece, of course!

Growler. [*Quickly.*] Do you think I'm crazy! [*Suddenly correcting himself,—in fear.*] No, no,—I didn't mean that!— Please, excuse me! [*Steps on the ulster and almost falls.* **Fred** *grabs him by the arm to save him from falling.*]

Fred. [*Holding him, and somewhat threateningly.*] Don't fall!—Now,—for the last time,—are you going to give her to him— yes or no?

Growler. [*Frightened.*] Yes, sir,—yes!

Fred. [*Releasing him.*] Very well!—Then I may tell Jones so?

Growler. As you please! [*Enter* **Jones** *and* **Hebe** L. 2 E.]

Hebe. [*Beseechingly.*] Uncle, dear!

Fred. [*To* **Growler.**] Now speak out!—Here's your chance!

Growler. [*Trembling for fear.*] Hebe,—for Heaven's sake,— to oblige me—say that you will marry that fellow over there! [*Points to* **Jones.**]

Hebe. Oh, uncle,—I'll oblige you with all my heart! [*Takes Jones' hand.*]

Jones. Yes,—so will I!

Growler. [*To Fred.*] Now, you have your wish!—I hope you are satisfied!

Fred. Yes,—thank you! [*Goes towards hotel* L.]

Growler. [*Breathing deeply as if in relief.*] Thank the Lord! Safe at last!--It's a terrible trial to converse with a lunatic!—You never know when they may get dangerous! [*Turns round and sees Jones and Hebe kissing each other.—Dumfounded.*] Hebe! [*Pulls them apart and steps between them.*] There is no occasion to play your parts so naturally as all this!

Jones. It's no play,—it's the real thing, uncle.

Growler. [*Perplexed.*] What! [*Hebe and Jones remain in conversation with* **Growler** *up stage, as if explaining matters to him. Enter* **Mildred** *from hotel* L.]

Mildred. My dear Fred,—Vivian asked me to give you this! [*Hands him a half dollar.*]

Fred. [*Joyfully.*] Fifty cents.

Mildred. Yes, for your contribution box!

Fred. Aunt,—this is kind of her!—Now, I'll pay a dollar,—for really I was to blame for it all!

Vivian. [*Entering from hotel* L.] No, Fred,—it was all my fault!

Fred. No, my love,—you are mistaken!

Vivian. Very well, then!—Just as you say!—In the future I will give in to you, whether you are right or wrong.

Fred. [*Spreading out his arms,—gladly.*] Vivy! [*She throws herself in his arms.*]

Vivian. And if ever a thoughtless word should again escape my lips,——

Fred. I'll close them with a loving kiss! [*Kisses her.*]

Mildred. Now you two are taking sense! [*Enter* **Harrison** *from hotel* L.—**Growler**, **Jones** *and* **Hebe** *have come down stage.*]

Growler. I can hardly understand that all this is reality!

Jones. Here is the proof, uncle! [*Spreads out his arms.* **Hebe** *crosses* **Growler** *and throws herself into them.*]

Growler. It's incomprehensible! [*Hits himself on the forehead.*]

Harrison. [*To* **Growler**.] I see one sucker got caught, eh?

Growler. Yes,—and that sucker is myself!

Positions:

Mildred. Fred. Vivian. Hebe. Jones. Growler. Harrison.

Curtain.

THE END.

www.ingramcontent.com/pod-product-compliance
Lightning Source LLC
Chambersburg PA
CBHW020242090426
42735CB00010B/1799